AS MY LEADERS GO... SO DO I

LAURIE SAYLES
www.lauriesayles.com | info@lauriesayles.com

A percentage of all proceeds will be donated to Dee's House of Hope - www.deeshouseofhope.org

Copyright © 2019 by Laurie Sayles

All rights reserved. No part of this publication may be reproduced, distributed or transmitted in any form or by any means, without prior written permission.

PurposefulTime, LLC
13216 New Hampshire Ave, Suite 10026
Silver Spring, MD 20914
www.purposefultime.com
timemanager@purposefultime.com

As My Leaders Go...So Do I / Laurie Sayles -- 1st ed.
3rd printing Dec. 2020
ISBN 978-1-7333550-0-1

DEDICATION

I dedicate this book to all the individuals who supported me through the recent attack on my life, way too many to mention. However, I must give sincere thanks to the leadership of Spirit of Faith Christian Center (SOFCC). Why do I say leadership, and not Pastor? It was the leadership of SOFCC that helped me through this challenge of life. I love Apostle Mike Freeman like a Father (even though we are both 60's babies), and Dr. DeeDee like a Mom, as both of my parents have been deceased since the 1980's. Pastor Dewayne Freeman, on the other hand, is like a big brother to me and he knows quite a bit about my journey, and Lord have mercy, he had to hear me talk and talk and talk during the attack (smile). Then there is our praying Pastor Deborah Grant, who I lean in on every time she speaks prophetically, and from whom I have learned much about praying. She has no idea how much impact she has had in my life over the past ten years. Yes, it has been ten years, January 2009 to January 2019, since I have been a partner of SOFCC, my church home that focuses on Faith, Family, Finances, and Fellowship.

Our mission statement is *"Loving, Serving, and Impacting Generations by Faith, In Excellence, One Life at a Time."*

Apostle Mike Freeman often says that he measures the success of the ministry by the transformed lives and not by its assets. I have made significant changes in my life throughout my life; however, I have been most fulfilled over these past ten years, as I am living my life by FAITH and RECEIVING God's love and protection. With that, I am becoming what God called me to be!

FOREWORD

I believe if anyone should tell your story, it should be you, because no one can tell your story as authentically as you can. I'm so glad that Laurie had the courage to tell her story, and I know it will prove to be a blessing to others that see their life's similarities through this body of work that she poured into.

There are valuable principles in "As My Leaders Go ... So Do I" that will help any reader, because principles will work for anybody, anywhere, at any time. Apply these basic principles to your life so the same God that Laurie trusted to change her story will guide you in making the necessary changes so your story can be one of victory too!

Dewayne Freeman
Assistant Pastor
Spirit of Faith Christian Center

ACKNOWLEDGEMENTS

These acknowledgements are not listed in any particular order.

As we would all expect, I must honor the Father, My God, My Lord, and Holy Spirit, as the Word of God is what I used to stand boldly during the biggest test of my life. Secondly, thanks must go to the Spirit of Faith Christian Center family, 1) Apostle Mike Freeman, 2) Dr. DeeDee Freeman, 3) Pastor DeWayne Freeman, 4) Minister Lisa Freeman, 5) Pastor Deborah Grant and the other leaders of SOFCC. I leaned in on every word they spoke because every word spoken by these awesome men and women of God who teach the Word in simplicity came from great examples to follow.

Along with having these awesome men and women of God, I was also encircled by other people of God who prayed, encouraged, trusted and believed with me during the fight for my life and the life of my business, which included the livelihood of others. My Civility Management Solutions (CivilityMS) team: Cheryl Thompson,

Dawn Ellis, DeAnna Boyd, Mario Walker, Norman Pryde, and Sandi Goins did a stellar job in keeping me and the company moving during this ordeal, and each of them is still with me, focused on the future of the company and the blessings we will all receive from seeing it survive and thrive.

CONTENTS

Chapter 1: Just Me 12

Chapter 2: Born That Way, Really? 20

Chapter 3: Not Just Men, But Now a
Christian Marriage - Wow 30

Chapter 4: Back to my Old Ways – Oh No!! ... 36

Chapter 5: Marriage Made Ez
Through the Word 44

Chapter 6: Always Been An Entrepreneur 54

Chapter 7: Pissed and Pumped
(*per Dr. DeeDee*) 62

Chapter 8: Don't focus on the Process,
but the Promise (*per Dr. DeeDee*) . 70

Chapter 9: Praise and Worship 78

Chapter 10: My War Room 84

Chapter 11: Leaning in on Others 94

Chapter 12: Faith and Patience 104

Chapter 13: Fight the Fight 112

Chapter 14: Don't Ever Give Up 120

Stories of Warriors on the Battlefield: 134

CHAPTER ONE

JUST ME

On Monday, January 2, 1961 at 8:55 am in the Cook County Hospital of Chicago, Illinois, a little stubborn, clumsy, tomboy girl was born. It is winter, so of course it is cold, and it is early morning. The celebration of the New Year has just taken place and my parents, Lawrence O. Sayles, Sr., and Lurlean G. Sayles (Ross) probably did not go out to the Tavern on the West Side of Chicago this year to celebrate with family and friends, as I was too close to being born. It was 27 degrees and the winds were a mild 5 mph, quite mild for Chicago; however, it was a great day for my parents, as I was their third child, and I was coming after a miscarriage. However, the real joy was hearing "It's a Girl!" When I was taken home to Chicago Public Housing Authority, better known as "The Projects," located on the West Side of Chicago, 1233 W. Roosevelt Road, I was introduced to my two older brothers, Marlon and Donald. My parents later had another child, my brother Manny, who became intellectually disabled during his infancy. It is unknown to me what actually happened, but I was told he was born sick and was given medicine stronger than what should have been given to an infant. Today, I am his legal guardian.

(1) Me and baby brother, Manny, I am his legal guardian (2) My tough brother Donald while incarcerated

My father was 50 years old at my birth and my mom was 39. My parents were both previously married, and my father was already a grandfather when he started his second family with my mom. I am sure they were the talk of the town in New Orleans when the Sayles families gathered to chit chat; she was 11 years younger than my father. I remember a time not long ago, when I went to New Orleans, Louisiana for my late half-sister's surprise birthday party. I loved my sister Shirley, as she treated me like her sister, not her little sister; even though she had two children older than me. She was admirable!

Although, I had known her all my life, this was the day that she would introduce me to her life-long friends. One of her high school friends, was bold enough to say in my face, "Oh, is this your little sister from the young (not nice word) woman that married your dad?" I didn't react, but I heard her loud and clear. Before I could think about being offended as this old lady talked about my mama, my sister graciously spoke over her and loved up on me more, with her old-time high school friend looking on. Let me move on before my 'feelings' come up on me again!

As I was saying, you see my father was previously married to a woman named Mabel and they had three children together, Lawrence O. Sayles, Jr., Lillian Sayles, and Shirley M. Sayles (Raymond). Each of my father's children had children when I met them, and many were much older than me. So, I was born an aunt! My mother was also previously married but bore no children and her married name from her first marriage was Ricks. My parents were the real deal as they were older, but my father enjoyed telling us the story over and over again that our mother had cried and cried saying, "I don't have any children," and "I am the oldest sibling and don't have no kids." Well, it was true, out of nine siblings, my mom was the oldest and she did not get pregnant until she was 35 years old, and as a woman during her era, who was from the south, this was shameful. So, I knew I was loved, as I believe each of us felt from our parents, but up until my mother's death, I knew that Marlon was my mom's special child. He was the first and wow, she must have been elated to have a child and he knew he could get anything out of her. Well, thank goodness I was a girl, because I got to spend more time with mom as she went about raising us as a housewife. As I grew older however, I did not like the fact that I had to go with my parents all the time, while my brothers were able to stay home and hang out. My parents always told me 'you're a girl' whenever I tried to convince them I could stay home too.

My dad was not a nice man, but he was in his own way. He was an old gruff and was a tough man like a black Archie Bunker, the character from All in the Family television series. My brothers were being raised by a man that understood his role was to provide for his family and spending quality time with them was not part of the plan. Did he do much for them to ensure they had what they needed? Yes, I recall him buying them a Moped motor bike while we were living in the projects. Heck, they were in grammar school and this Moped was great for when we went to the country to visit Uncle Clarence and his family, but not for residing in the projects. It was a total distraction for them, and my brave brother Donald skipped school to drive it down State Street, a main street in Chicago, during school hours. Was he noticed? You better believe it. He was picked up by police and mom needed to pick him up from jail. As it turned out, picking up Donald from jail was a normal way of life for my mother. Donald was my brother that sought out trouble regularly, and I am sure my dad died not knowing how much he was in and out of the hands of the police, because mom took care of it before Dad arrived home. Marlon, the oldest, and I always knew about Donald's trouble with the police because he was already home from school before us on way too many occasions.

My parents were both from the South and migrated to the North during the 1940's. This era is best known as the Second Great Migration, as it was the migration of more than 5 million African Americans from the South to the Northeast, Midwest, and Western parts of the US. It began in 1940, continued through World War II, and lasted until the 1970's. They moved to take jobs in the burgeoning industrial cities in the North. My Father worked as both a Hat Blocker and a Janitor and my mom worked in Jewish homes as a cleaning lady. Sadly, I don't know the story of how they met. However, I do recall the story of 'how' my mom discovered that my father was bald, as all his brothers were. She narrated the story like this *"It was a full moon night, and we were strolling down the street and as your dad was walking me home, I reached up and snatched the brim, decked out with a feather from the top of his head and to my surprise he had a bald top, but the moon light shined off of it so beautifully."* She always giggled and laughed as she reminisced on this memorable moment.

My mom was born Lurlean Gladys Ross, in a Sharecropper family that picked cotton for a White man that owned the land on which the family lived. They were in Stoneville, Mississippi based on her birth certificate, but she referred to Leland as her birth city; however, this town is in the heart of the Mississippi Delta. Farming is still the basis of the local economy, as it was since before the Civil

War. I also know that my mother did not go beyond the fifth grade in elementary school before she had to return home to assist her parents with raising the children and maintaining the household, which was quite common for young black children in the South. My mom and her sisters loved going to the Taverns on the West side of Chicago, where they landed from Mississippi.

I have learned that Leland is in the heart of blues country, having produced several national and regionally famous blues musicians, with Trail Markers of "Highway 61," and is the burial place of the folk artist and blues musician James "Son" Thomas, and blues musician Johnny Winter. However, I also learned that one landmark in Leland called the *Rex Theatre for Colored People,* dating back to 1937, was prominent when she was only 16 years of age. Seemingly, when she got older, she became acquainted with the city of Greenville, MS, which is 8.4 miles away, as I often heard her discuss Greenville when she mentioned her cousins.

When my grandparents passed away suddenly, one right after another, all nine (9) children had to go and be with my Grandad's sister. This was the beginning of the end of my mother's time in Mississippi as they did not get along, and she decided to pack her bags and relocate to Chicago. This Aunt utilized my mom and her siblings for all of the outdoor work, including picking cotton, while her children got to stay home. Since she had girl cousins who had already left Mississippi for the big city, she felt she too was ready. My mom became the Harriett Tubman of her family and returned to Mississippi throughout the years bringing one after another North to Chicago, until they were all residing in the same city as she was.

My dad was born in 1910 in New Orleans, Louisiana as a twin, but his brother died shortly after birth; however, he had a total of 6 siblings. The family was devout Catholic and at a very young age my father's oldest sister taught me how to read the Rosary, which was required while being at her home in New Orleans. They also were a family that truly believed in discipline and structure. Whenever I was around them, it was really clear how they expected kids to behave. My dad's relocation to the North was due to domestic violence between him and his first wife, Mabel. He told me that he found out she was cheating on him and they fought, which led to him being arrested. Since the marriage was over, his oldest sister recommended he relocate and he chose Chicago, Illinois, which opened the door for my parents to meet, and I am truly glad they did!

Although I could go on and on with stories about my parents, my upbringing and my family life, that is not the intention of this book. However, I first wanted to lay some groundwork of how I came to enter this world.

(1) My mother and her sisters (2) My dad and his brothers (3) Marlon, Donald, and Me with an Aunt (4) My Parents

CHAPTER TWO

BORN THAT WAY, REALLY?

As far back as I can remember, I was a tom boy and followed behind my brothers as much as they would let me. Heck, my oldest brother, Marlon had no choice as I was his responsibility if I was outside. One dreadful game that I had to play in order to fit in with the other kids, was "catch a girl, kiss a girl." Oh my, I hated this game! You see, I was a long-legged skinny girl and I could run, and catching me was not easy, but if one of the boys got lucky and caught me, I would make the effort to punch him in his face when he tried to kiss me. Duh, Laurie, that was the point of the game...silly me, right? Also, let a boy grab my hair, which was long and thick. Well, I would turn to punch him immediately, no questions. Oh, and don't let him say anything to me that I deemed disrespectful, my reaction was strong and mighty as I had a loud voice and cursed too well for being a child. You see, the indirect teachings of my two older brothers and dad were both good and bad – smile. As Apostle Mike says all the time, "more is caught than taught."

I wanted to do whatever my brothers did, and I tried over and over by climbing fences, climbing trees, playing sports, playing with trains and race car sets even though I was doing this when they weren't around, and much more. Due to this behavior, I was known as a tom boy, and took no offense to the title as it is defined as "a girl who enjoys rough, noisy activities traditionally associated with boys." Heck, I couldn't even hide it because I was always reporting to my mom in need of a bandage and some Mercurochrome, that red stuff. Furthermore, my father's reputation was that you didn't mess with Mr. Sayles. As he entered our project complex, the guys would part the crowd to let my father through and when we became homeowners, no one would sit on my dad's ride, as it was known that he would check you! You see, this was training from my father and my brothers. You weren't allowed to disrespect me. They were not allowed to show weakness and they taught me how to protect myself by throwing punches when I felt the need, not swinging my arms uncontrollably, like a girl!

With that, I took no stuff off boys, but I had a weakness for girls, and I gave in to them all the time. I recall a close friend that took total advantage of me. She was the prettiest girl to me and was my very close friend. She had beautiful black long hair and a dark bronze complexion but was not as tall as me and carried the best name, Christine. She was conniving, however, if she asked for my candy, my money, my anything, I gave it to her! I recall us walking home together behind my brother, Marlon, as he had to keep his eye on me all the way home. He, however, did not know that I was being bullied by Christine, who I simply loved. What I know today was that I simply just enjoyed having a girl around me because I had no sisters in my home and my friends who were girls were fulfilling that gap, but with wrong thoughts at that young age.

"I am a girl," and as a black girl this was something I dealt with up into my adult age because I had no hips or butt. How is that? It made no sense whatsoever, as both of my parents were clearly black and yet, I was left without the same appeal of all other black girls around me, including my family. Boys and girls would tease me and say, "Laurie so skinny she can stand behind a tree and no one will see her." You know, kids can be so mean. Much of who I was represented a push back from boys and a love for girls. I was the only girl in my home and desperately wanted a sister and would ask my mom for one often. She would always answer, "Mama can't have no more kids, baby," but it didn't keep me from asking whenever my brothers left me out of their activities.

My friends were my everything. I played with them. I helped them. I supported and gave to them. I was a true friend. Let me discuss one game I simply loved to play, house. I always played the role of the Father. Heck, I was so good at it as a child, that my friends requested me to be the Dad, no matter whose home we were visiting, including family. Well, sadly, in most cases I was the only one with a Father in the home, which of course meant I understood the difference of the roles, and they didn't. I had a take charge, get it done attitude, along with being taller than most my age. This led to why I felt I was born a Lesbian.

But, to further define the reason I felt that I was born this way, once I began to read, I would go to my brothers' rooms, as they were older, and of course they had books and novels on sex...straight pornography. WhooHoo, I had hit the jackpot I thought, and I was only 11 years old, a child. There were only a few Hustler and Playboy magazines, that came later, but they had books that shared stories of ladies, and then men having sex. The odd thing would be that I did not get excited, nor was I interested in the reactions of the male anatomy. I was only engaged by the way the woman reacted to what was being done to her by the male. This was more confirmation that I was born that way, a lesbian, a dyke, right? All my life I was interested in making girls, ladies and then women feel good, even sexually.

When I became a grown woman, these types of stories of reacting to boys or girls helped support the theory that "I was born that way," and I finally embraced that I wanted to experience this life. When I joined the United States Marine Corps at the age of 20, I had a talk with myself in the mirror and I was able to tell myself, "I don't like you," and this caused me to make a change. I was living much of the street life before the age of 21 and I knew it was taking me nowhere. I had to ask myself if jail was an option. One of my brothers chose the life of crime and served two-terms in prison and I was all too familiar with the court system for the poor with no lawyer, and the visits to the jail house. Being 21 gave me the title of adult, but I didn't feel that at my parents' home, so I decided to join the Corps and change my life. It did just that for my life, but during that time my lesbian desires could begin as I knew I would be surrounded by many girls that were like me. The Corps did not disappoint in this area. Now, homosexuality was against the rules of the military, so I did something major to prevent being caught. I married a man! Yes, I did it. We went to the courthouse to make ourselves legal, but we never had sex! We were roommates only. He had sex with men, and I had sex, as a bisexual female, with whoever I desired.

After being with men and living a bi-sexual life for many years, once I decided to get out of the Marine Corps, I immediately gave all my attention only to women. You see, being a dyke was fulfilling to me as I really was sold on being born this way. I went on living my life, as I did not care about what anyone else had to say about it. So, the transition in changing my appearance began after I got out of the Corps and along with that, I became comfortable with revealing male mannerisms to the public. It was refreshing, so I thought, as I was headed back down the path of 'why' I left Chicago in the first place. Upon returning to Chicago after a full transition to a Dyke, I picked up old habits and took on new street hustles to supplement my income (you must wait on another book for these details). This was all under the belief of enjoying my life!

Well, after finding a woman that I referred to as my wife, we left Chicago to once again "improve" my life and Palm Beach, Florida was the landing. We bought a home together in the 90's, and could have adopted children (hence, my lack of understanding of equal rights in the 2000's) if we so desired.

We attended a store front Catholic church where homosexuals, transsexuals and divorcees, all the unwanted Catholics in the Roman Catholic Church attended. And yes, I did say store front as this church was established by two priests that were a homosexual couple. Going to this church and sitting under the Word penetrated my heart and despite the congregation and my celebrity status, I was moved to leave the lesbian life.

Celebrity status you may ask? Yes, I was a male impersonator on stage for close to five years. I performed under the stage name "Lare Gaye" and performed as Marvin Gaye, Luther Vandross, Will Smith, and Smokey Robinson to name a few. At that time, I was the only woman that was doing 'drag' on stage professionally, meaning I was being paid. Most had no idea I was a woman, including the gay, feminine men that would come up to me after the show only to be disappointed to find out I was a woman and had a wife. At one point, the MC of our troupe asked me to come out at the end with a gown on as he wanted to 'wow' the crowd with the fact that I was a woman not a man. Yes, I was good at performing. One day my Pastor, Dr. Mike informed the congregation that a man who chooses to be homosexual needs to just 'act' like a man instead of 'acting' like a woman. I whooped and hollered as I knew the truth to that statement he made. I was acting like a man for way too many years and was now using the Word to be the woman God made me to be.

Then the day came that I just couldn't hold it any longer and I told Kathy, the woman I considered my wife, that I was leaving the lesbian lifestyle. She had me take counseling sessions as I, too, was confused over why for the past year and a half, I had been pulling away from her and feeling the desires for a man, a husband, children, etc. What was major about this is that I went to see a psychiatrist for six sessions, just for her to say to me "looks like you have already made your decision." I was told I was going through a mid-life crisis. Well, I wasn't. It was real. My heart had changed, and I couldn't change it back. So, when I was resolved with knowing that I could not live out my life with Kathy, I was asked by a co-worker if I would like to stay at her home in an extra bedroom. I accepted and moved in with Robin and her young daughter. Robin had a room with a twin mattress on the floor, a dresser and a mirror. This became my home for over 6 months or so as I worked out what I would do with my life. Since Kathy and I were homeowners, leaving my home and all my belongings was necessary in order to maintain some peace within myself. But, there is one thing that I was doing at this time, when I laid in my room at Robin's home, that I wasn't fully aware of. I talked to God, not prayed, I talked with Him. At this time, I didn't know this was praying, fellowshipping and placing a demand on his Word. I would speak to the Lord about my confusion, real confusion of who I was and that I didn't understand what was going on with me, but I knew I had to change.

I would go in depth of how I was feeling, what I was dreaming, what I was thinking about, which were all new thoughts and ways in my life. These so-called, one-way conversations were building the relationship with God that I never had, and it was always such a rewarding feeling to speak to Him out loud, may I add. You see, it was my private space in Robin's home, and she may have heard me chatting away, but I only focused on who I was talking to and that was God. Yes, he can call you unto Him, but we must listen to Him whether it's loud and clear or that small voice.

(1) Just Me (2) My party swag (3) My professional photo as a Drag King, "Lare Gaye" (4) Playing Bid-Whist ... a favorite game

AS MY LEADERS GO...SO DO I

CHAPTER THREE

NOT JUST MEN, BUT NOW A CHRISTIAN MARRIAGE, WOW!

After leaving the homosexual life, I returned to the DC Metropolitan area and started my new life as a heterosexual. Upon my return, I once again stayed with an old friend, Toni, who is still a friend to me today. Having her in my life has been my blessing and connection to the DC Metropolitan area. I recall my first encounter with a man that was interested in me. Oh my, I was all dolled up with my new hair color, make-up, long earrings and even more jewelry. Changing my hair color to blonde was instrumental because I had seen myself with a short barber hair cut for almost 15 years. Even though, I had changed internally, I looked the same in the mirror, so I had to make an external change. As I sat talking to this handsome man, I needed to excuse myself; I had to go to the bathroom. Well, what came out of my mouth was ridiculous, but relevant to who I had been. I said, "I need to take a piss!" His face told me "uh oh, that was all wrong," and he responded, "that is odd for a woman to say that." Ump, I just got up and went to the bathroom. Needless to say, it was too early to engage guys and this beginning had an abrupt end.

I was just beginning the journey of dressing like a girl again ... note blonde hair color, earrings, makeup, and heck I even have on a skirt (lolol)

I gave myself some time, but I did go out to the local clubs in Temple Hills, Maryland just to get myself acclimated to being around straight or heterosexual people. You see, the church was still not set in my heart, so I went about getting knowledge the way I knew, the streets. I always went out by myself to check out the scenes, and I have been doing that all my life. Even as an extrovert, I found this easier to have complete control over my night, especially living a secret life to others.

One of the following men that I gave some time to, asked me to marry him. However, my mistake was marrying him simply because he accepted who I used to be. This was a big deal for me! So, I thought, I should snatch him up as not many men would accept the life I once lived as a lesbian, or worst yet a dyke, feeling like I was as much of a dude as dudes themselves. In this case I was. I gave 10 years of my life to one person, yes, one person. That was a huge change for me as I had never done that before. You see, I was a player; always had been and not because I tried to be, but because it was easy to be.

What I remember is that I met a man that attached himself to me completely and became my close friend. However, after faking my past life with him, as if I had been a straight woman before meeting him, I decided to put the truth on the table. He grew quiet and decided to take me home without any discussion, and when I said "say something" he said nothing to me, and I do mean nothing. After he dropped me off, I expected to never hear from him again. I recall crying out to

God as I felt abandoned and that no man would ever be able to accept me because of who I use to be. I wanted to become transparent and free in my new walk, and I refused to continue my life in a lie.

But, to my surprise, he called, and I was so nervous that I almost dropped the phone. As stated earlier, I was accustomed to having whoever I wanted in my life ... heck I was fine in the eyes of ladies and gay men. The fear of being told that he could not handle my past life and that he could no longer see me or be my friend was a blow I wasn't ready to receive. But, guess what? He wanted to see me and chat. With joy I agreed to meet with him. He begins to tell me that he knew nothing, I mean nothing about the LGBTQ community and that he cared too much for me to keep me out of his life. So, we continued dating and, oh my something happened that I would have never expected. I got pregnant! I couldn't believe it. There I was, approaching the age of 40, and pregnant, what the what? Well, as I displayed my consistent dismay, he finally said to me "why are you so shocked, you are a woman?" I laughed, and thought, oh my he so doesn't know me! Well, he committed himself to me and we got engaged. Although I had a miscarriage, the marriage moved forward.

I stayed too busy during the years we were married by pouring into my jobs, getting my hustle on with the Boot Camp Outdoor Fitness Program, my first side hustle; Melaleuca Marketing Representative, my second side hustle; and returning to school to complete my Bachelor's degree, which was one of the top three reasons why I returned to Maryland. However, he was in and out of jobs, even though I saw him graduate from law school and the bar exam after several attempts. Since I was the primary provider, and came from a unified financial home lifestyle previously, I never saw myself as a "woman" taking care of a "man," I was just doing what I do.

Nonetheless, I believe he became depressed and since I was so busy doing, I didn't notice. The fact that he was not a strong communicator caused life to just go on as normal. But one day, I had an epiphany and it was not good for him as I thought "why?" Why am I living this way? I did not have love or respect for him. I was not attracted to him, and furthermore, I saw him as weak. Because of how I was raised, and who I became as an adult, I never respected him the way a wife should respect her husband. The Bible says, "A man should love his wife and she should respect her husband." With that, I looked in the mirror, as I had done two other times in my life and spoke to myself and said "You can do better than this" Additionally, I knew I was not first in his life, his son was, yet I was understanding of it, as he didn't care to take care of me or ensure that I was safe and provided for. I told myself, "you can do better than this." The beginning to the end of the marriage began this day.

You see, I became a student at University of Maryland (UMUC). This school focuses on seasoned/older students and grants college credits for work experience. With that, I went on to obtain a Bachelor's in Social Science with a minor in Strategic Entrepreneurship and Leadership. When I travelled to College Park, Maryland from Washington, DC, I would listen to Christian radio and Dr. Mike of Spirit of Faith Christian Center (SOFCC) was on the radio. I began to listen to him whenever he was on and found myself both entertained and moved by his teachings. I would go to class late in order to finish the broadcast that ended at 6 pm, which was the time class started. When I did not get what I needed from the 1st Christian church I was a member of with that husband, I went to a Bible study in Ellicott City, Maryland to simply check out the church. There I went up to receive Holy Spirit. Shortly thereafter, I became a Partner and brought my then husband along with the desire to save the marriage that I wanted to stay committed to based on the Word.

Immediately after becoming a partner at SOFCC, I scheduled a meeting and met with Pastor Dewayne Freeman at the Brandywine location. We both went and Pastor Dewayne asked for a second meeting with him only. I don't know today if that meeting ever took place. I continued to come to SOFCC, and it has now been over ten years and oh what a blessing to my life. Before we were separated, I often questioned whether or not I was meant to be with a man, or if I should return to dating women.

CHAPTER FOUR

BACK TO MY OLD WAYS – OH, NO!

I returned to my old habits and displayed a different person to my husband, and while I was travelling with Toni, my old buddy from Chicago ... he moved out! This was actually a good thing as I knew as long as I stayed the "good wife" he would sit there and take from me for the rest of his life, because I made life much too easy for him as the man, a married man. Now, before I start this chapter, I aim to share the enemy's work and his trickery!

I was with this man for close to nine years and had been faithful, totally faithful; however, as soon as he left the home, all of a sudden, repeat that after me "all of a sudden," my past showed up and they each said "I have been looking for you." I had a Facebook account for my businesses in Fitness and Melaleuca. In its early days, Facebook was not the social site that it is today. However, the first lady that found me on Facebook was someone that married a man that I introduced her to years ago back when I set up dates for ladies of the night. Yes, I was a pimp, or a madam since I am a woman - smile.

The second lady was the love of my life (I thought), and I challenged my own life for over two years having an affair with her, as her woman/husband was a cop! But, oh no, I didn't care, I was tough enough to handle that and I spent time with her whenever she gave me her time, which was often. Well, when she found me on Facebook she said "Crystal, her old friend told me that I will find you on here!" I must say this was exciting to have her look for me as she crushed my heart over, and over again (well, I let her), but I was madly in love with this woman and she was NEVER FREE for us to be a couple. I was always her young stud (another name for the tough lesbians) on the side. I fell for it for many years and actually practiced abstinence (no sex) for over a year just to keep from hurting other women along the way, while I waited for her. All along she was lying to me. She is the woman that gave me the name Lare. You see, she was ultra fem and I was still too feminine when I met her and she helped bring out the dyke side of me for everyone to see, as I was accustomed to only behaving that way behind closed doors. When I showed up right, (in her eyes), I was named Lare, and it was a name of affection to me for all the years I used it.

The third one was a Puerto Rican woman who was my side chick in Florida where I lived my last days with Kathy. I met her after one of my performances as Lare Gaye and took her home that night and the affair began. I cared about her as she had some struggles in life and I was there as much as I could be considering we both were in relationships. However, she later told me that she was hurt when I ran off and left for Maryland, but I failed to realize how I had also impacted her life, and at that time I didn't care. I just needed to run from that lifestyle and follow where God was leading me, without any real knowledge of "what was happening to me."

The fourth one was 'crazy' no, really, and I had to get that sista out of my life. You see, I was falling back into the mindset "well, I guess I was born this way." It was way too easy to pick up women, as all I had to do was 'show up' and I would certainly get a number or a one-night affair at the minimum. This woman wanted to take full possession of my life and jealousy and stalking began. No matter what, I wasn't going to put up with that behavior in my life. Don't try to keep track of me when I am not with you … are you crazy? Now, I had learned enough about how the enemy works, and even with the obvious timing, I still fell for it hook, line and all.

The fifth one was the most comfortable in returning to the lifestyle, as she gave me all of her time, living only 15 minutes from my home. You see, we knew each other from the past, but we never dated, and I was friends with her and her lover. Even though she was attached at this time, I was a way out of that relationship as she was not being treated well, so she said. But, once again I am fooling around with a chick that has a cop as a partner. Don't ask me, but it's as if I had my own death wish attached to this lifestyle (hehehehe). Thank you, Lord, for keeping me. She became wifey quickly in my home and did all the right things to pull me in and yet, I had to tell her, no, I could not settle back into that lifestyle because I had total condemnation when I was alone with my thoughts. She was devasted as she too was a Christian and yet, had no condemnation and could not understand why I couldn't just get over it so that we could be together.

The sixth and last one I will discuss that came into my life during this one year of separation stayed in my life into my singleness and was the most dangerous. The one thing that assisted me in distancing myself from her was that she did not live in the DC Metropolitan area, and that helped me push away from her. She brought so many qualities to me that I desired in a person that I knew could be a strong bond, or a power couple. Like others, she too was a Christian, grew up in a very Christian lifestyle, and her mom did not approve of a lesbian lifestyle. This woman was tall, dark and drop dead gorgeous and carried herself like a queen. She was married, as I was, and she moved out from her husband, as her deeper desire was to be with a woman, a wife! Despite how much she affected me, I pushed her away ... only to have her show up at times with phone calls. Each time she called, it affected me, as I thought of how good my life could be with her, but yet, good is not me being my greatest and I opted out.

So, I did fumble back into the life of Homosexuality, only to realize that I couldn't! I started by stopping attendance at weekly service as I knew I would be uncomfortable with my choices and the Biblical teachings I would hear at SOFCC. You see, Holy Spirit was working me over with condemnation and I finally honored it and brought it to a halt. So, when I returned, to SOFCC to my surprise the ministry had started FREE (Fully Recovered Educated & Empowered) which was established just for me it seemed! This area of ministry was for individuals that were being challenged with homosexuality and other sexual perversions. I attended the meetings regularly with Minister DeeDee Cutler at the helm, and since many were younger than me, I attached myself to her leadership and grew in understanding clearly, that "no, I am not born that way." I had to fight the choice of returning to that lifestyle or returning back to God.

Me and old friend one month before she died of breast cancer; but, I was beginning transition back into my old lesbian ways – notice the stance!

Even today, I still have tendencies that are a reflection of a tomboy, lesbian/dyke because it is a part of who I have been, but I use it now as a businesswoman or when I go to Department of Veteran Affairs (VA) hospital/clinic, and when I walk the streets in the hood. For example, as a businesswoman, many men already have a certain thought whether it's "Ump, she's fine and I want those digits," to thinking, "Okay, she has no idea what she's doing." No matter what his thoughts may be, I have a firm handshake and I look them directly into their eyes. I stand against any man disrespecting me as a woman business owner in every way. I am a professional. That means covering up my assets to ensure I do my part to cut out any confusion. I am determined to ensure that they don't see me as a sex symbol. There are way too many times I see my sisters show up with tight beautiful dresses (put a jacket on it), or way too much cleavage and heaven forbid when the dress or skirt is too short. Although, I no longer have desires ... thank the Lord, I can still see it! But, let's be clear, when a man is getting a business card from a woman that is presenting ALL that, he can be a little confused on how to proceed. I know how I use to think!!! I have had a few guys go there, and I get close to them and professionally check them each and every time.

Another example is when I am walking into an environment that is male dominated or when I am walking in the hood, passing by my brothers on the street. I immediately change up my swag, no matter what I have on to make sure they see that I am not that 'chick' that they can say anything to. I demand my respect with my appearance I present to them. Amazingly, it works most of the time, so with that, I continue to use it. You see, it can be very intimidating to go to the VA hospital and see all these men staring you down like you are a piece of meat. Now, I am not intimidated, which can be part of the problem because the one that decides to test me by being disrespectful will find out that this beauty has got some things to say and checking him in front of his buddies is too easy for me. As a woman that loves God now, I have become what Proverbs 31 says about me and I do walk in it proudly; however, I tone it down in order to assist the men at those moments.

I can admit that what is most disturbing for me during these challenging times walking down the street is when I pick up my old walk (pimping), as that is a huge no-no for me! Yes, it gets me through some environments easier, and I know how to add a "what's up" with a nod of the head to really shut them down. I typically giggle after I get to my location sometimes as that nod throws the fellas off every time ... sweet! However, when I wear certain shoes, like gym shoes or flat boots I do need to monitor how I am walking, so I use my imagination that some fine dude is checking me out (smile). But, let me share a story of why.

You see, Ms. Sandi is a lady and she looks the part all the time. This was the woman that introduced me to Christ beyond religion. Well, she was my co-worker and she spent time during lunch breaks with me and without me telling her, she realized who I was at that time. One day we decided to leave the building and go to lunch at the Union Station in Washington DC. As we were walking and talking, she asked me to look down at my shadow, I said "ok." After staring at my shadow, she then asked "do you see what I see" and I said "no, what are you talking about?" and she continued to have me stare at my shadow and finally after she realized I did not see what she saw she boldly said "you don't see yourself pimping?" LOLOLOLOL ... she is too much! Now, Sandi is a homegirl from Chicago, so we can speak the same language, pimping ... really? But she was right and at this time I was in transition and I had not purchased new shoes, as I owned many already. Even though I was living a lifestyle as a dyke, I had mad shoe swag! Well the next day she brought in a big bag of shoes. Needless to say, they were all heels and I still own a few pair today! I say all of this to say, I watch my life now to ensure that I am presenting myself as I should to the world, including how I act.

CHAPTER FIVE

MARRIAGE MADE EZ THROUGH THE WORD

I was sold out on what Pastor Mike said to us as partners and living a holy and righteous lifestyle became appealing to me as I wanted to please God. With that, I cleaned up my life and began to attend service weekly, to include Bible study with Pastor Dewayne. One day Pastor Mike asked us women to ask God to return us to our virginity, and I did it! I spoke with God on this matter as I wanted him to renew me in preparation for my Boaz.

You see, I was practicing abstinence now, and in the Word daily. I was studying the Proverbs 31 woman and receiving what God said about me for the first time in my life. It was both rewarding and refreshing as I was strong in my stance of not having sex until I was married. As Pastor Mike would say "no ringie, no dingie!" Also, Pastor Dewayne got bold enough to use his body for the motions of having sex and shared how we would talk to God during our fleshly sin and think to ourselves that the Lord should understand our heart. This was rewarding to be walking out a life of living holy unto the Lord with my body, even though I was meeting males that were interested in me. I was bold and told each gentleman early in their efforts of talking with me that I desired to be married and that he was going to be the only one that I have sexual relations with. They were turning away, one after another, and I was good!

Now, I am someone that is comfortable with online dating sites as I never cruised the site but allowed men to see me and contact me accordingly. I've also posted pictures that reflected me as a lady, a Christian; hence, I had my body covered and no side/back pictures. I was clear that you had to be a man that not only loved the Lord, but went to church as I refuse to be with someone that was not going to get up and go to service with me in order to live out this life of joy, peace and strength in the Lord. With that, I got a hit from someone that was divorced for a long time and desired to be married. We met and then he began the work of courting me and honoring my desire to not have sex before marriage.

He attended church with me and before marriage Pastor Mike announced in front of us that someone in here has fallen in love. Well, he had no idea that the man sitting next to me was courting me heavily and he was expressing his desire to have a wife. Pastor noted that he had never made that statement before in church, but he also expressed his feelings on falling in love saying if one can fall in love they can fall out of love. Nonetheless, both of us agreed later in life that it was a divine comment from my Pastor. So, when he gave me an engagement ring, I told Pastor, and it was only 30 days after meeting him. You see, Pastor Mike and Dr. DeeDee's parents were both married within a short period of time, less than 45 days and these examples I had before me were still together after 50+ years of marriage at that time.

This man proclaimed his love for God in most, if not all, of his communication. A friend of mine, who worked in law enforcement, asked to vet him. We reviewed each other's credit report, and underwent counseling sessions independently and together as a couple. We were married in 60 days! In retrospect, I must say that it was quite upsetting to learn that after 6.5 years of marriage, the online court system offenses would reveal much of who I married that was never reviewed by the law enforcement contact that I knew. She had asked for his name, age, and social security number when I told her about him. However, when I returned to her after learning some very detrimental information that was available 'before' we were married, her response was "I didn't have any charge against him to validate digging deeper on him." Well, my immediate feeling was "why did you ask me for information if you couldn't do the research." Worst yet, this information is available online and all you need is the name of a person. So, ladies and gents, please, please check out your state court records on anyone that is interested in being in your circle.

Nevertheless, our story was fascinating to people and everyone was happy for us, or at least I thought. One thing I did was take this man to meet two couples that I admired and held in high regard and the wives are close to me. They later told me that they felt a certain type of way, but did not share it ...devastating for me, as my goal was to get their input on the gentleman and the reason for the meet and greet in the first place. Do realize I am a grown doggone woman and I have lived a full life at this time. In the past, I didn't care what you felt about what I was doing. But now, as a Woman of God, I have learned to trust in others that care about me. Consequently, they both know to NEVER do that again and to be honest and forthright with me ... don't just desire for me to be 'happy'!

Having a man that understood the importance of studying the Word, going to service, and paying tithes was more important than money. Whereas, I am a hustler/entrepreneur and getting money to survive has always been possible and available. More importantly, being someone that served in the Corps, being a team player is major for me. Well, he presented all these great attributes, to include being healthy and someone that works out. One thing I did in order to ensure that I would attract my Boaz, I followed the scripture of "writing the vision and making it plain." I had a nice list of attributes that hung on my bathroom mirror to state what I needed and wanted from my husband. Well, he checked off all of them except one before marriage. The reason I didn't know it until after we were married is because it was about him being a 'big baby.' I wanted an alpha type man that could be emotionally sensitive to laying his head on my lap and needing affection from me in a motherly fashion. Well, it started off that way!

We got married on the beach, a lovely place it was, and we often talked about walking the beaches of the world together. Now, when we went to get the license in Florida, which is where he resided at the time, I recall his excitement so much so that he wanted us to get married on the spot when we obtained the license. The city employee informed us that she could read us our marriage vows right then and there ... I smiled and said 'no' as we are sticking with the planned date. He was the greatest in this area as he took care of all the purchases and basically planned the wedding with some assistance from his daughter. All I had to do was show up, including buying my dress! Now, some may find this odd, but again, as a woman that had dressed like a man for many years and yet had a failed marriage already under my belt, him picking out my clothes to ensure that I was always attractive to him ... was ideal for me.

Some of the most disappointing findings were that he really did not live a healthy lifestyle and I was eating right and working out with a vengeance, as I owned Semper Fi Fitness at that time, which was an outdoor bootcamp program. Also, he felt he 'knew everything' and that included the Bible. I often wanted to lend my thoughts on a matter, and he would have total disregard and worse yet, it would be on a subject where I was the expert between the two of us, like fitness! Being with someone that is controlling in areas where they are weak is never a good situation, as I like succeeding in everything that I do. As a Marine it was required that we operate at 110%. Well what do you think I had to do as a Woman that just happened to be Black ... more like 130-140%.

I received continuous appreciation from other women telling me that I had a great man and husband. This was always pleasing and satisfying as I knew the steps and the sacrifice I made unto the Lord. He would often tell women that they should sit down with me and get insight on the steps I took in order to prepare myself as a wife for my Boaz to show up. I held quite a few of those sessions. Actually, the most memorable was with his daughter. She was 21 when I met her, and she was sweet and seemingly innocent. After getting to know her, asking her to move in with us, and sharing more of myself, she began to tell me more about herself ... and she was not so innocent! But she was a young lady determined to live a great life and since she was mature beyond her age, as I had always been, we became very close, and praise God, we are still very close today.

Also, one lady from church, who is now happily married, came to me one day in service to share how she admired seeing the two of us worship God together during Praise and Worship. I sat down with her one day earlier in the service and told her my testimony and shared pictures with her of 'who' I used to be, which was to give her even more encouragement of her Boaz showing up. You see, she is a beautiful woman inside and out, and I knew that she would soon be found and become a happily married woman, and she did. I can tell you that she now blesses me with great uplifting inspirational words every day since the attack on my life. How awesome is that ... reaping what I sowed, but now I am the single woman.

Regarding employment, I was fortunate to be employed by a company as a Project Manager overseeing $11.5 million worth in contracts with up to 128 personnel. Another manager of the company had a position become available on a contract and, to my surprise, she offered my new husband a job. She smiled at me and said "well, he is relocating here right?" So, she worked her magic and he was now a government contractor, learning much about the work world that I was in as we drove to and from work together every day. It was a sweet set up to be able to talk shop with him and yet not be working directly together. Shortly thereafter, that same individual was able to get his daughter on a contract and more than doubled her salary. She was ecstatic! The great thing was that neither of them reported to me and there were no conflicts with us all working for the same company.

We became financial supporters of Marriage Made EZ (MMEZ) at the highest level at SOFCC as we wanted to sow into other marriages being great. We attended many of the sessions, and I attended some by myself if he was not up to it, but I knew things could be better. After I became aware that the issues concerning me were not changing, I inquired about marriage counseling to ensure that we stayed focused on having a great marriage. He did not agree. So, I went by myself and once again I was sitting with Pastor Dewayne discussing 'how' did I get back here again. Totally different, but similar, and the main concern was his financial support to the household. You see, since I lived a lifestyle as a lesbian or dyke, I carried the role of the man and I did not know how to write out a 'honey do list.' So, if something needed to be done in the home, I would just handle it and make the call as I am not a handy woman, at all. But this was not the case as much as it was the need to have financial support in the home.

As stated earlier, I was operating an outdoor fitness program when we met, and it was clear that I was an entrepreneur because I discussed my goals and aspirations as any couple would do. But, when I established Civility Management Solutions (CivilityMS), a government contracting firm, I had his approval. God gave me wisdom to seek advisors, and he was one of them, but the Lord directed me to do many things that were ideal. For example, obtaining a SCORE mentor to walk me through the process. Well, one of the first tasks was to come back with my spouse to confirm that they would understand the demands that were to come if I started the business. We did that and all was well and the efforts of attending training at the procurement technical assistance center, along with SCORE was my focus. Oh, and don't let me forget to discuss the need for networking and networking and more networking in order to become known in the space. As folks do business with people they know, like and trust!

Several referred to my husband as "Preacher Man" as he would teach and speak on the Word of God if you gave him any of your time. He also believed that we would write books, minister and speak to large audiences on 'never giving up on God's word," especially as it concerns to marriage. Why you may ask? Well, we are both baby boomers and we had entered into our 50's in this marriage. So, even though the marriage was not at its best, I continued to trust God and spoke over him with the Word despite how he was acting, which was the main strategy of Dr. DeeDee with Pastor Mike. She trusted God for her marriage, and she used the Word on another level that is not often taught ... It doesn't matter what it looks like, do your part as a child of God and pray, trust, and wait for the manifestation. Better yet, the examples of doing this were right before me ... Glory!

AS MY LEADERS GO...SO DO I

CHAPTER SIX

ALWAYS BEEN AN ENTREPRENEUR

The thought of establishing CivilityMS came in 2009 when I began government contracting for a small minority owned business. The desire to have my own money came when my parents allowed me to start 'babysitting' in the projects with young ladies that had babies. During my youth, while residing in Hillard Homes projects in Chicago, I asked my mom if I could begin babysitting within the building. At that time, I just saw an opportunity to make money; however, there were many young mothers with little children, and since our 22-story project building was one of two that had 10 apartments on each floor, there were many potential clients.

When I was working for these young ladies, I was between 8 to 10 years old, but these very young mothers saw my maturity, and they had to meet my mom before I could be in their apartments. Now, this babysitting was for short periods, like 1 to 3 hours to simply allow the mother to go to the store, run errands, or go on a date. However, my mother took a liking to one of the young ladies and she was only three stories down from our apartment on the 10th floor. My mom would allow me to stay longer hours with her children for her to go to work in the evenings, and I am sure some of those long hours were for her to go on dates. I recall meeting some men that brought her to the door. But I must admit that I was so happy about this relationship, because I was attracted to her as she was a beautiful young woman, but somehow, she had the misfortune of having two small kids and no husband. I spent a lot of time in her apartment as I somewhat became her little sister, and like family.

The biggest joy I had working for the young ladies of the building was having spending money. When I wanted to buy candy, I just went and bought some. When Christmas came, I recall being allowed to go downtown by myself to purchase gifts for my family. Imagine that, a young 8-year old skinny poor girl getting on a bus and going into downtown Chicago to shop by herself! I had travelled with my mother many times downtown and sat with her at Woolworth's counter and drank milkshakes often enough. So, I knew the drill. She trusted me and I was so proud to have my big brothers and my parents open presents from me on Christmas, without any knowledge of what was inside the wrapping.

The next experience of making my own money was when we moved to our new home on Bishop Street in Chicago, the sticks, as the projects folks called it. I quickly recognized an opportunity during the summer to sell candy, as the closest store was at least a 30-minute walk. At the young age of 10, my mom once again agreed to me getting my hustle on and she took me to Jew Town, a Jewish shopping area where you could cut deals on any purchases that were made. We went to purchase the candy at a wholesale price.

I recall on one of our trips my brothers both came along and as we had packed up the car with all the shopping from Jew Town, my mom made the mistake of hitting a car as she was backing up. Now, she was an excellent driver, and despite the 11-year age difference of my parents, my mom taught my father how to drive. She panicked and as she thought to get out of the car, my brothers screamed for her to just drive "Mom, there is nobody there, just drive." Well, my mom was much of a goodie two shoes type of lady; however, she was in the car with children that grew up on the streets of Chicago, and the two in the back seats ran the projects we lived in. So, she hesitated, and they kept repeating "mom, go" and she decided to listen to her sons and pulled off.

We giggled about this as she drove off and got further and further away. As a family, we had gotten away with something and had convinced mom to participate. This was way cool to me as a little girl to see my mom misbehave. This still brings a smile to my face to think my mom allowed us to 'push' her to break the rules. As we, her children were already breaking the law when the opportunity presented itself. Then, shortly after entering high school I found another hustle, being a distributor, not a pusher, but a distributor! As I stated, I have always been an entrepreneur. This lifestyle of hustle all ended when I decided to join the illustrious United States Marine Corps, which was a good thing because like most criminals, I was going to get caught if I didn't stop.

It was good news when I left the street life and joined the Corps and I was glad to have gotten out of Chicago. Well, only to return after ten years or so. Yes, the hustle met me at the airport upon arrival and I pushed back for quite some time in order to settle in on a job, which I always had but as always, I wasn't making enough money for me to live my life. I wanted more in life, I always did, and I recall telling my father during my high school days that I would travel, own nice cars and big houses and in his fearful wisdom he said "Baby girl you dream too big." You see, being around since 1910 to the 1970's was painful times for many blacks, and especially those with no education. My dad only thought to say that to protect me from what he believed the 'white man' would never let me have. There are songs that take me back home to living in the projects in the 60's that bring tears to my eyes when I think of my parents, their struggle and who I am today ... Glory to God:

- Sam Cooke "A Change Is Gonna Come"
- Marvin Gaye "Inner City Blues" and "What's Going On"
- Curtis Mayfield "Pusherman" and "Brother's Gonna Work It Out"

Beyond that, I fell into another means of hustle and it all started from two lovely women I met out at a lesbian bar on the south side of Chicago. This was a spot that I would never have anticipated to become a lesbian bar, as it was in the hood on 79th, but it was a cute spot and again, I operated in bravery most of the time. So, I would travel from the North side of the city where the gay/lesbian activity was more acceptable and there were many restaurants and bars/clubs waving the multi-colored flag that represented the LGBTQ community. But I was from the South Side and hence, I traveled to support the sista that was bold enough to open this spot. I had a good time with these two young ladies that were basically bi-sexual and wanted a good time (read between the lines); however, one of the two stayed attached to me and once again I was operating dangerously being 'me.' She had a boyfriend at home, but oh, I was so stoopid!!

But, to get down to it, she was a 'dancer' via a pager with a coded message. After having some interesting and at that time exciting times with her, I found myself setting up dates between men and women, and a new hustle had been birthed for me. However, I somehow met a woman by the name of 'Zori' and she was a white girl that was attending college in Evanston, Illinois, as she wanted to be an FBI agent. However, she was a Dominatrix (a dominating woman, who takes the sadistic role in sadomasochistic sexual activities) before and after class in order to pay for college. I don't recall where she was from, but it wasn't Chicago, and I became a safe haven for her and she then introduced me into her world and, oh my! I was amazed to see the amount of money that men and women paid to be screamed at, cursed at, humiliated and sometimes beaten, but no sex! One home I went to with Zori had to have four girls, so I invited my woman, Kathy, who was a tall 6'1" white woman with an athletic swimmer's body. The ladies were all asked to wear spiked heels and short skirts and sit on bar stools and humiliate the husband. Yes, we worked through the wife who gave all the rules, direction and the cash for the 1-hour service. Easy money, we each thought. At one point, one of my ladies (workers) told me about some geeky boys establishing an online sex shoppe. This was new, very new, but I was interested in meeting them and checking it out and when they met me, they asked if I would be willing to manage the girls. Of course, my answer was yes.

These two geeky white males had the technology and the cash to make it happen, but no management and leadership skills. This is where I came in, and together we made lots of money just having fun and doing what we liked doing. I handled the ladies, their schedules, their paychecks, etc., and, of course, picked up some new friends, you know what I mean. But I did bring in my girl, Zori, who needed to get a job that was going to provide her with a W2, as she was preparing to graduate soon and was really desiring to become an FBI agent. I knew if she made it, they would have themselves a great agent as she was smart, fearless, and very cunning. I liked her a lot and wished nothing but the best for her.

Well, this crazy life needed to end and again, me and the mirror had a conversation after I got into a relationship that I felt serious about and both Kathy and I left Chicago and I got a fresh start in Florida. Only to find myself in another hustle ... Drag King! Being a Drag King was easy for me, and it was legal. I was good at acting out being a man on stage and performing hit songs that made folks holler, scream and throw money. Driving up to night clubs and seeing my name in lights always, and I do mean always, brought a big smile to my face. Not to mention all the perks that came along with this lifestyle on stage! I always had options to how I would end my night, if I was on travel and away from Kathy.

The establishment of CivilityMS was a natural flow for me, as once again, I saw an opportunity and, as always, it had landed right in my lap. I began to study this world of business and realized this was my wealthy place. The fact of being a woman, a minority and a veteran now became an asset in a way that I never knew ... and at times I was upset about not knowing of it earlier. Why, well, how could I not know about this type of business, as it was always a fit for me. As a military person you are always preparing for some new challenge of either a new rank, a new duty station, etc., and government contracting is exactly just that. Each contract has a beginning and an end that will bring a change.

(1)Me and the CivilityMS team celebrating 4 years in 2016 (2) Me and the CivilityMS team with Pastor DeWayne Freeman of SOFCC, Amber BabyGurl, David Harrington,CEO of Prince George's County Chamber of Commerce, Todd Turner Council Chair of Prince George's County and Colin Byrd, Council Member of Greenbelt, MD

CHAPTER SEVEN

PISSED AND PUMPED
(*per Dr. DeeDee*)

My First Lady, Dr. DeeDee Freeman, of SOFCC, said openly in service one Sunday while my Pastor, Dr. Mike Freeman was in the hospital fighting for his life, that she was "Pissed and Pumped." This is one of the biggest tragedies she had experienced. Now, I grew up Catholic and even though a lot was said before and after Mass because once you had communion, it was back to sinning. I never ever would have expected to hear such strength to being Pissed and Pumped to be said in a church service, I mean while she is teaching/preaching in church. Like, for real? Well, Dr. DeeDee said it and I felt every bit of her anger and her fight to win the battle that she was encountering. I applauded her words, the volume of her voice, and the tone was all on point, because I too was pissed and pumped that Satan would come for my Pastor. What the what ... was my thought!

You see, when the enemy recently came for me ... it was with a vengeance, and it was through my husband. I too was feeling every bit of being pissed and pumped at Satan, and if you were anywhere near me to hear the volume of my voice and the words coming from my mouth, you knew it! Now, I had to get some control over my words, and still feel that I can be challenged in this area due to the level of the attack. You see, as a city chick, I know some words, but they are definitely not Godly. As I was pissed and pumped, I had to keep saying the one scripture that I often said to myself as a black woman entrepreneur ... "no weapon formed against me shall prosper." It was just more challenging as I had to realize that I had been sleeping with the enemy.

It was as if someone from the Lifetime Television program had asked me if I wanted to become an economic, emotional domestic violence victim and allow my story to be aired, and I agreed! You see if you followed the enemy around (who knows how far back), you would have a film recording of a great love story that was about sacrifice, growth and determination but ended in the works of pride, jealousy and ego. Whereas, if the film recording was of me, it would be good material for a Tyler Perry or Bishop TD Jakes movie as a married woman's Christian walk was being challenged by the one that was to protect her. My team at CivilityMS, and I questioned when the enemy was sleeping because we were managing daily attacks during all hours of the day and night ... it was mad crazy! Why, because we all knew this person wasn't going to go hard after anything, well, so we thought.

The attacks of Satan are tricky and if you listen to him ... he will rule and reign in your life. So, I began to notice jealousy, but I certainly didn't want to think I was once again experiencing a jealous husband, that's just crazy. Well, when I was appointed to lead the Veterans Ministry at SOFCC, with no request from me may I add, but I had the right connections for this area of ministry. I looked at it as God's blessing of raising me up as I had to now attend all services on Veterans Day and better yet, stand before the congregation. Now, this was his heart's desire, never mine ... I'm a businesswoman and only want to write the checks, as Pastor requests. Either way, here I go, and I have no pictures or video from these moments in front of the congregation because he clearly was sitting their stewing, instead of celebrating.

On the way home he only told me what I could have done better or attacked what I wore, etc. I listened constructively in order to improve, again, I was a Marine, I can handle criticism in order to improve. Then comments and behavior within the office began to show apparent jealousy and ego and my team thought to not say anything to me because this was my husband. However, I often stated that no family or friend working for CivilityMS would be favored over another in order to prevent water cooler chatter. Oh well for that, as we were not all in agreement!!! My enemy opted not to care about this desire of mine, and all other corporate employees refused to say anything because he was my husband!

The day I knew I was sleeping with the enemy I was told the following: *"If you don't give me a percentage of the company, I will take you to court and the judge will determine whether I get 49%, 35% or 25% of the company."* I turned my back to the enemy that was speaking and began to pray in tongues until I fell off to sleep. You see it had been a long day and it was close to midnight. I am 100% owner of CivilityMS, and this was never questioned by anyone and it clearly simplified the government's certification as a service-disabled veteran, woman and a minority owned business. Plus, his life story was to do ministry, never entrepreneurship. But I went to bed knowing that I had a problem on my hand. From that date he got more aggressive in stating what he would take from me as we're married, and he was clear of how the law says he gets half!

I walked around the home binding the enemy no matter who was present and went through the whole exercise of opening the door and speaking to Satan and telling him to get out of my house and that he couldn't have anything that belonged to me (another lesson from Dr. DeeDee). Well, I learned that my home security system was not properly named as my company pays the bills since I have a home office. Once I called them, I learned that my name wasn't even on the account and when I told them it needed to be corrected, I learned that I needed the password. What password, I thought? Well, I inquired with the enemy and he gave it to me and when I called back a few days later or so to the security company I was told that the code was incorrect. What? Well, I tried it once again in my home and when his phone rang upstairs and he responded with one word answers I realized the security company called him to inform him that 'someone' was calling to get access to the account. I panicked and left my home immediately and went directly to my office and noticed I had left my home in house slippers and no coat in February. This was the beginning of a nightmare!

Once I left my home, the enemy began to put in place a lot of resistance for me to simply return to my home to include changing the locks on the doors. I was forced to find another place to live and I stayed in four different homes during a six-month period. Mind you, this was all happening as I ran my close to multi-million-dollar company, to include sitting on panels and acting like life is normal. The emails, the phone calls, the text messages were unstoppable for five months and they were vile. Heck, the way my Pastor found out was because the enemy wanted his tithes and offerings back from the church.

As the Pastor asked me about this matter, I did not know what the email entailed, but I knew what type of communication I was receiving, and I only hoped the Pastor wasn't reading the evil I was reading. I didn't know this person any longer, as Satan had taken full control of his thoughts, which created terrible actions out of him. Unbeknownst to me, this was just the beginning of a long saga of destruction, lies, stealing and social media attacks. It was painful as the legal system supported each effort of the enemy that was lying and claiming criminal charges to include charging me with 2nd degree assault with an attempt to have me imprisoned for up to 7 years (Maryland State Law). As you have heard me say "I have always been an entrepreneur," and that would be legal and illegal activities. So, everything in this city 'gurl' was fighting the idea of going to jail for something I had not done, especially since I had cleaned up my life. Now I am saved, Holy Ghost filled, fire baptized, and a legal beagle. You see, I enjoyed who I had become with a 'renewed mind' in Christ and I had to fight to stay the course of the Lord, as Satan was always talking, and it was not Holy talk ... as expected!

I knew this was more than I could handle by myself as the other responsibilities in my life were not going away; survival as a single woman; running CivilityMS; being a speaker upon request and being a leader and a friend to my peeps. So, I did what was natural to me and leaned into my sisters and brothers that could help guide me through this attack on my life and my business. My BFF, DeAnna Boyd was truly my ride or die (live) in the courthouse. She went with me to ensure I was never alone, and it was needed, and I didn't know it. Doing things by myself is a norm for me, and I include others just for more fun and joy usually. But this was for me to feel the strength of knowing I was not alone in the battle, physically, and she had to stay girded up as well. The enemy sent him after her as well and she stood strong as he spoke to her "You're going to be fired," with a voice that I could not even identify. Amazingly she was going through Iyanla Vanzant's program during this time and it was for her, and now I realized it was also for the Lord. For the first time after knowing her for almost 20 years, she prayed in Jesus name ... Whaaaattt? Bam, what the devil means for evil, God can turn to good!

One of the people I spoke to often during this time was DeeDee Cutler, a retired police officer. DeeDee was my consultant in the process of dealing with the legal system and I leaned in and learned all that I could about 'how it's done' and did it. You see, I had a brother who spent years in prison, and I did not like entering court rooms, especially being black. So, that unease had to be nurtured and I needed to be taught how to behave, but I got it! Another person I spoke to often was Fredricia Cunegin for spiritual food and real sisterhood discussions. She led me on fasting and praying with her and always, I mean always, had a scripture for me to focus on to help me through. Another person was Angela Douglas who still to this day sends me daily texts or Facebook messages. Now, this sister admired a couple in church as they did praise and worship together and desired marriage with the same love for God. She is now living with what her heart desired and I congratulated her getting the man who became her husband. Today, she is now nurturing me in my singleness. This shows how God's principle of "sowing and reaping" can pay off in ways beyond money. She is truly a blessing to me! Oh, and by the way, these are all SOFCC partners and awesome women of God.

Before we move on into this book, I need to be clear that I have forgiven my enemies for every time they listen to the devil instead of God. You see, this is the basis of Spiritual Warfare, who are you listening to? Within five days of being outside of my lovely home, SOFCC had Holy Communion and I was not challenged at all, as I knew enough Word that I must forgive. You see, forgiveness is for you and your walk with Christ. I refuse to let Satan end my relationship with God because some would understand 'why' I would. I had done it the 'right way' this time, and yet, I got a sheep in wolves clothing. Forgiveness will always be necessary!

CHAPTER EIGHT

DON'T FOCUS ON THE PROCESS, BUT THE PROMISE (*per Dr. DeeDee*)

When I established CivilityMS, immediately the enemy began his tricks and even though I had made the introduction of my company to my current employer, I had to experience some backlash from the forward movement in my career. I was selected to serve as a Leadership Consultant with NASA Headquarters after going to an interview for an administrative position that was available on the contract. You see, when a small business in government contracting is experiencing a decrease in revenue, one way that keeps employees employed is to place them on contract. I was fortunate to be one of those employees; however, instead of being offered a position as an administrative assistant (for which I was over-qualified – at this point of my career), they called and offered me the position of overseeing the mentor protégé program they provided to federal staff. I was shocked as I had no idea what this would entail. Bottom line, I had the life and professional experiences of being able to do this job and sadly, another person lost their job in order to bring me on board.

I was elated, as I love a great challenge! However, as soon as the negotiations began, I was majorly disappointed as I desired to take the position as a 1099 employee so that I could work under my company and begin to get paid for past performance (experience/revenue). Well, they wouldn't allow me to do so, but yet the President and CEO had previously told me to 'make this happen,' in order to help CivilityMS as a start-up business. So, after losing that fight with dealing with the #2 person of the company, I was offered a salary that was significantly less than the white male that was fired from the position. Their argument was that I lacked the proper certifications, but my argument is that their customer requested me to take on this position as I brought more to the table than the person that they currently had in the position – obviously. But, despite my argument on this matter, they refused to increase my salary, but worst yet, my offer letter was even less than the agreed amount via the phone call offer. Whew, I was hot and experienced emotional cries in my car every morning for weeks prior to heading up the elevator to master this job that NASA personnel requested me to do for them. Well, I did a great job (of course) and I made great relationships. Since leaving NASA, my company CivilityMS has continued to seek opportunities to support the mission of NASA and providing executive coaching has been one area that we have supported them. How did I get through this ... well, I didn't focus on the process after I got through my anger, but focused on the promise of God and took advantage of the experience and I am still reaping a harvest from the solid relationships I established by showing up and getting it done.

Immediately after this contract, I was requested to send my resume to fulfill a position on a contract with the VA. WhooHooo, I thought. Now, I can work for my company and become a sub-contractor supporting another company who has won the award at the VA. I hired myself as the Facilitator to manage an acquisition support contract, only to get on contract and the prime company had a Program Manager (PM) that was not efficient in the position. Within 48-hours the government was telling me that they wish I was their PM, well, I thanked them for the compliment and said, "that is not possible as a second-tier sub-contractor." The government did not settle with that answer and within two months I was assigned as the PM overseeing another companies contract; however, I rose to the occasion and once again was in a financial fight. I requested an increase in my hourly rate, only to be told 'no,' once again. At this point, I am feeling some kind of way about this consistent mistreatment, especially because I am clearly a bad, bad chick that can handle the business of others, but not being compensated as such.

Again, I had to lean in on the Lord and not focus on the process but realize that my company was now obtaining the experience and revenue in the bank to move CivilityMS along in its growth. Not to mention, I was able to work from home and manage the contract and that allowed me to attend training, attend outreach sessions with the government, and being able to keep my presence in the right places to become a known business owner in the industry. Constantly walking and talking "no weapon formed against me shall prosper."

When I was sitting at my kitchen table paying myself minimum wage ($7.50) while having a sub-contract within the Federal Government that was a $4 million, 5-year award, I had to keep my mind on the promise. Why, you may ask ... well because my company had only grossed $265,000 at this time from this $4 million-dollar contract. Despite meeting the veteran owned small business and receiving all the promises of mentoring my company into federal government contracting, the leadership decided to unfairly split the revenue with CivilityMS. Once again, I had to deal with not being treated right and yet, I knew that I had to stay the course of marketing my company to others, including other small businesses. You see, teaming on a contract is expected and a necessary force in federal contracting, but many small businesses suffer at the hands of more mature companies that choose to take advantage of them in some way. When you're small you're not in a financial position to take anyone to court to challenge the documentation that has been signed, so you take the loss and move on. However, CivilityMS was fortunate to have some revenue, as I know many companies that don't receive any of the work after helping another company obtain the contract due to their relationships or their expertise.

In order to jump now to my most recent attack from the enemy, I knew that I had to focus consistently on every promise of God that states the following:

- I am the head and not the tail
- I am above and never beneath
- I am the lender and not the borrower
- The wealth of the wicked is being transferred to me
- Do not fear, for God is with me
- God will make a way of escape
- No Weapon formed against me shall prosper
- God will never leave me nor forsake me
- Be angry, sin not
- I can do all things through Christ who strengthens me

These are quick remembrances that I walked and talked daily. When Dr. DeeDee shared with us to not focus on the process, but on the promise ... I received! I took this in and told myself often, while I was depriving myself a 'life' as a grown doggone woman in her 50's, that I need to stay the course. I will win in the end. You could have not told me in 2012 that it would be 4.5 years before I would see a profit in my company ... why, because I was entering a space that I was familiar with and had great relationships, so I thought. You see in Government Contracting, your relationships are working with tax paying dollars, and should be held to high regard on how these dollars are spent.

Since I experienced my company going from $178,000 in 2016 to $1,700,000 in 2017, I knew then that I was winning the battle of staying the course of building CivilityMS. I just didn't know that the worst challenge of my life was around the corner. It came, and when it did, I was challenged with not focusing on the process initially, as I had to be in the process daily to protect my life, my freedom and my company. You see, I was being criminally charged by my husband, yes, my husband, my holy ghost filled, fire baptized husband. Being served by the Sheriff on a fraudulent charge of a 2nd degree assault was devastating, as it was all a lie! So, now, I was in a process of obtaining an attorney, numerous court appearances, countless courthouse visits, blocking social media attacks, investigations by the government, reading harassing emails, texts and listening to harassing voice messages, and much more. My enemy was real and as stated before when Satan has been given permission to dwell, he will take you to another place that you may not be able to return from. The man I knew was gone, I didn't know his voice, his actions, or his motives. Ok, I knew he had become jealous of the movement of my life, I knew he had a big ego and was da man in his head, and lastly I knew he was full of pride ... but, I still didn't think he would ever be capable of doing what he was doing to me, for sooooo long!!!

It was challenging to not focus on the process, but I did keep fighting for my peace, my joy, and my faith in God as it did not look like I was winning, at all. There were folks telling me to get new attorneys as they were not moving matters fast enough, and my enemy seemed to have grown 10 arms and 10 legs because the attacks were happening fast and furiously. In the end, I had 4 fraudulent criminal charges (two 2nd degree assaults and two theft) that I had to manage while trying to run a business with approximately 20 employees and 8 consultants. You see, the legal system is established where you can file a complaint against a person at the commissioner's office and provide no evidence, none whatsoever. It is just a story on pieces of paper. Heck, you can even go online and type it out and take it to them. Either way, if they believe your story, they swear you in and charge the individual ... just like that! So, I got four fraudulent charges placed on me that I had to pay retainers to an attorney to now show evidence that I did not do the crime. This is awful, simply awful and as a woman having a man act this way toward you is simply outrageous and way wrong if he is your husband. His job is to protect you!

My pastor teaches us that "my response, is my responsibility," and even though I learned this while serving in the Marine Corp, it was the revelation of being told by a man of God that gave it the substance that I live by more today than ever. But, oh my, it was being tested during this attack. The Assistant Pastor, the older brother of my Pastor, DeWayne Freeman, taught on "Handling Offense" during Bible study for several weeks on Wednesday some years ago. This teaching changed my life, as I was one that would get offended and feel disrespected by someone and it would weigh on me for months to years.

Whereas, now I don't allow people to 'offend' me anymore, as when it rises up in me, I quickly acknowledge it and change my thinking. I mean change my thinking every time it raises its ugly head because I must get some things done and I can't do what needs to be done if I focus on being offended by anything or anyone. I now use it as fuel, to press forward so that I may be a blessing to myself and others. I had no idea that having that teaching many years ago would be so beneficial in my life now in both my business and personal life.

CHAPTER NINE

PRAISE AND WORSHIP

I was a party animal. I mean if the clubs were open, Laurie was in the house! I enjoyed dancing, cocktailing and partying as a young woman and since I have always been an entrepreneur ... I was there as a distributor as well. Growing up in Chicago, we had "House Music" which was created inside a warehouse in an industrial area of the city, and I was in there during my High School years. This was the beginning of me sneaking in dances with girls in a dark corner of the club as this was a homosexual spot, and straight folks invaded it when it was discovered. Frankie Knuckles, the Godfather of House music was the D.J. at that time in 1977. I had no idea that I was at the beginning of a wave of music that would travel the country, especially amongst the homosexual community.

Not to mention, the best place to make that money was in the clubs. I was always prepared, and my reputation was well known. So, when I gave my life to Christ and I learned about gospel music, praise and worship, etc., I was all in! I did not have to be taught how to dance unto the Lord, as I was always dancing with no return. No, correction, I had a return, but I can assure you that it was not anything I needed. Being able to take someone home after a great night of dancing with them was not to my advantage, thank God I escaped sickness and disease.

Praise and Worship is a way to keep peace and joy flowing through you! You see, God is with you when you honor him in giving him what he deserves. But, let's be clear, not all gospel music is good music and I have learned from my church, SOFCC, to listen to the words, and if they don't line up with the word of God, I turn it off, change the station, or skip to the next song. A good beat was all I needed back in the day, but now a Word of God is what I need, and I must receive it in the music I listen to as I honor God and give him praise. Dr. DeeDee always says that praise will avenge the enemy and I can tell you that when my attack came, I got 'turned up' on my praise and worship as I had to get through these seconds, minutes, hours and days of torment.

Women Walking In The Word (WWW) Session with Dr. DeeDee ... Minister Lisa pulled me up front for prayer

Some of my favorites songs during this time were the following:
- Brian Courtney Wilson - "A Great Work" and "My Witness is in Heaven"
- Sinach - Any song she sings
- Yolanda Adams - "In the Midst of It All"
- Jekalyn Carr - "You Will Win"
- Tamela Mann - "I Can Only Imagine"
- Kem, Patti and Ronald - "Jesus"
- Tim Bowman - "Better"
- Anita Wilson - "More Than Anything"
- Chris Tomlin - "Good Good Father"
- Helen Baylor - "Testimonials"
- Tasha Cobbs - "I'm Getting Ready"
- Marvin Sapp - "Close"

I cannot sit down on God, and I haven't since I got saved in 2000 as the first church, I attended was all about the music ministry. They allotted for you to be over an hour late to church because the first 1.5 hours of service was praise and worship, no, really it was. So, when I left that church for a new Pastor the songs were totally different, so I sat and read the words as they went across the screen and rocked to the beat and not too long thereafter, I had understanding of their praise and worship. It was truly to speak with God on what his Word says, and the ministering of those word took my praise and worship to what it is today, powerful and freeing. I don't care if everyone in the service is sitting in their seats, I will be up on my feet as I know how great the Lord has been to me.

You see, being raised Catholic meant that you did not get Gospel music, just hymns. So, I recall when I got introduced to gospel music in 2000 that I was told by Ms. Sandi to attend an evening service that had Donnie McClurkin in the house. Well, that did it for me as I could relate to his story on the challenge of homosexuality. With that, I purchased every CD he made and listened to his music in the traffic heading to work every day and was blessed. Then when I was visiting with one of my cousins I shared with her how much I was enjoying Donnie McClurkin and I mentioned how great my church was in praise and worship and when I mentioned the Music Director's name she had to inform me that he was a gospel artist. I actually sat there debating with her that he was not; he was our music director! She finally broke it down to me and explained in a worldly matter by bringing up Motown artists so I could understand ... shameful now! If I mentioned his name here, everyone would know him, lololol. In closing she told me, "Girl, go and buy some other artists other than Donnie McClurkin."

Hence, the new world of partying for me became Gospel music! The Bible tells us that if the people keep quiet, the stones will cry out and praise the Lord, well, not on my watch. I feel like no one can out praise the Lord with me around, as I have performed on stage as Lare Gaye in Chicago, up and down Florida, Washington, DC, and New York and today I still use those skills ... lip syncing. How, well, I lip sync songs I cannot hold the note on and get it in, like Jekalyn Carr and Yolanda Adams! I love many of their songs, but I don't have that voice (I am alto/baritone); however, me and the mirror praise the Lord as if I am in concert somewhere ... too much fun!!

CHAPTER TEN

MY WAR ROOM

Dr. Mike and Dr. DeeDee invited Dr. Caroline Leaf to SOFCC and one of the messages I got from her and her teachings is that 'we must think about what we are thinking about.' I live this way now, and with that, I am able to redirect my thoughts as I ask myself at times about why I am thinking on something negative more than I should. For example, while going through the attack of receiving emails, phone calls, text messages and defeat in the court room, I was challenged with thinking about going to jail for seven years for the charge he placed on me. I heard him say it over and over on voice messages, read it daily in the enemy's communication, and when I had defeat in the court room time after time, I began to think, "is it possible, can I go to jail?" One defeat in the court room was simply trying to get the judge to state in my protective order "DO NOT CONTACT ME" but since this was a civil matter of marriage, it was very difficult. Heck, the judge gave us both access to the marital home, despite the craziness of our lives at that time. Really?

I meditated on it long enough to bring suicidal thoughts into my mind. First, I saw myself needing to turn back to becoming a dyke, and everything that life represented for me. You see, I was not going to jail and becoming some wife to some dude (dyke) ... oh no, not me! With that, I began to re-engage my mind on how I used to be, and how I carried myself. Not long after accepting this necessary step, my mind went suicidal. As I was not pleased with being locked up ... especially for something I did not do. You see, in my worldly days, I did some stuff as an entrepreneur, that would have me behind bars still today if I had gotten caught.

Now, to imagine going to jail for something I did not do was more than a notion for me. I first began to see myself in a cell, alone, and I had created a sharp edge that I could use to begin cutting my wrists and laying there to listen to the blood droppings. As taking my life became a way out, I found myself driving on the highway and looking for a means of suicide. What I saw on the side of the road I thought could be used to ignite the engine of my car if I ran into it. After a week of these awful thoughts, I knew I was letting my mind go too far. I hollered, and I do mean hollered in the car, "Oh no devil you are already stealing and destroying, but I will not let you kill me as I have too much, too much to live for."

That evening, I went to trusty YouTube and listened to some of Dr. Caroline's podcasts to bring my attention back to the methods of fighting this fight against my mind. When she came to SOFCC, I purchased the "Switch on Your

Brain" book and was totally sold on her medical and spiritual insight of our walk as Christians. So, I went through a program online to learn more and yet, during this attack, I had fallen off from these teachings, as I was so overwhelmed with what was happening to me and busy, and I do mean busy with attorneys and my team fighting the daily activities of my enemy. Since the attack, I purchased her book on "Think, Learn, Succeed" when it came out, and I have it in my home gym accessible while I do my cardio workout. I am always asking God to bless me with wisdom as he gave to Solomon, and that is directly connected to my thinking and I got to have wisdom as a serial business owner. To me, learning is imperative for change, which always leads to growth in our lives, but be mindful of what you're learning.

For example, I have much love for Joyce Meyers, as she has been a blessing in my life much longer because I watch the WORD network and I have listened to her over the years since 2000 when I got saved. I particularly appreciate her teachings on "The Battlefield of the Mind," and she has a program on the Word network under this title, as she was one of the first Pastors, I heard speak on the importance of renewing your mind. Now, at SOFCC, this is discussed as much as any other form of pastoring from our leaders. I often call upon the scripture that says, "Let this mind be in you, which was also in Christ Jesus." A true-life saver for changing my thoughts because after I say that, I then begin to think on God's Word.

Since there is much documented information that I must share with the world on the attack of the Devil, I wanted to only share in this book some of the aspects of what Spiritual Warfare looks like ... as it is real. Again, I don't and never knew this person until 2018, and oh my, Satan is one that you must keep out of your lives. Below are some pictures of the damage to my home that was made after the enemy was told by the courts that he had to leave, and once again, I was pouring out money to fix things. You see, I stayed with a few folks. One of them was Dawn Ellis, as she was renting my home in Bowie, and amazingly, before I got back into my home, I needed to go back to my old home. How humiliating right? Well, my neighbors were now seeing me again after being moved out into my half-million-dollar home, but as stated earlier, NO OFFENSE ... just was going through!

(1) Mountain of clothing, personal, jewelry, and miscellaneous items that were piled over 4 feet high (2) Demonic messages posted on front door for anyone to see (3) My gym (4) A closet in master bedroom was being destroyed over a 3 day period, each day the holes got worse

(1) Door damage from kicking in the door to my dressing room, (2) Dismantling office space and throwing items all over the floor (Note Dr. DeeDee's book FOCUS is in the pile)

When I was living outside of my home for approximately six months, whatever space I had became a War Room. I had post-its up everywhere to help keep my mind right. Now, I was fortunate to settle into two locations that I had total privacy, including my own bathroom. So, when I was in their dwelling, I dressed up the bathroom, the dresser, the entry way, the exit with post-it's that gave me the strength of God's Word. Right now, they are still up in my master bathroom in my home as they have continued to give me support as I fight battles of building revenue back into the company to save the jobs I have offered to my peeps.

AS MY LEADERS GO…SO DO I · 91

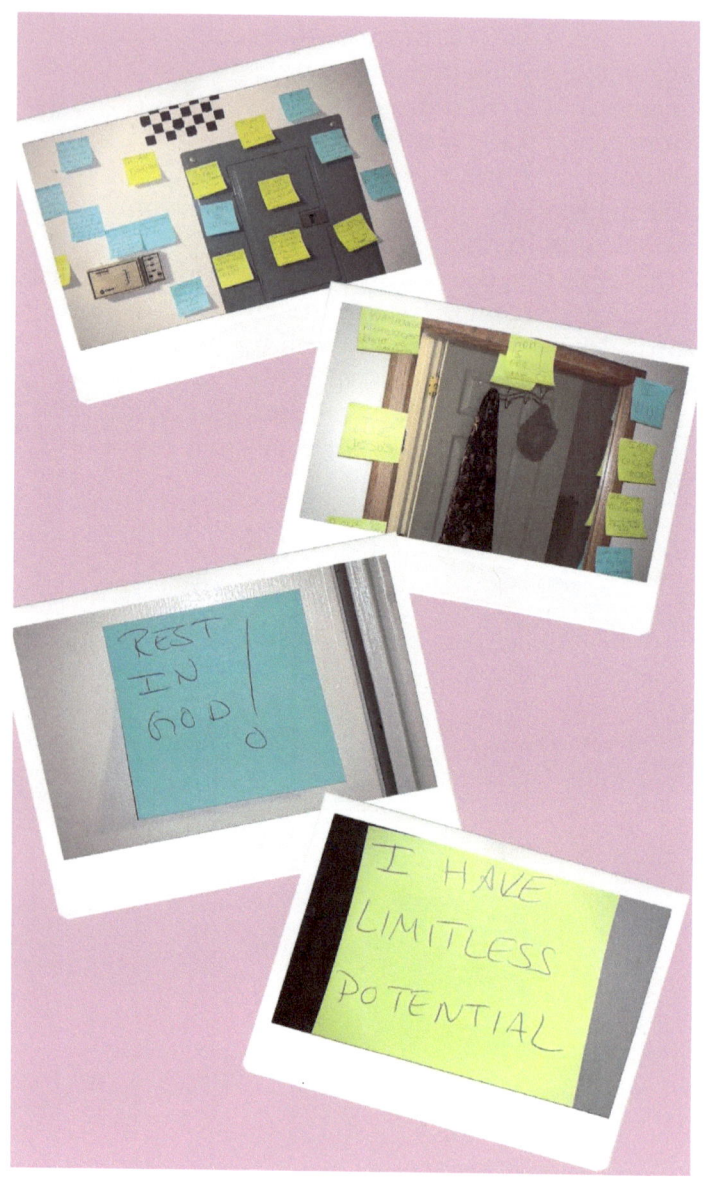

Post-it's in dressing area and bathroom

Most people are aware of Domestic Violence, but many may not understand what it actually means. Even though my enemy claimed that I assaulted him twice, when I didn't, he obtained all the benefits of a victim in counseling, including a free attorney for divorce and other resources. But, after a year of going through the attack on my life and the business, I called House of Ruth myself because I acknowledged that I too am a victim, despite how victorious I knew I was in Christ. I wanted some counseling and at this time, I knew I needed to stop talking to everyone that had been in this journey with me and go and get professional insight from Domestic Violence counseling professionals. Oh my, what a blessing it was for me to have six sessions with a millennial that brought out of me words that I had never said out loud. Yes, both refreshing and freeing for my spirit to say out loud "I have been such a fool!" You see, I had been a fool as I allowed so much in this marriage that I should have handled immediately as it was happening; however, I was being naïve and trusting God for changing his heart, and removing his lazy Spirit, as this was not a representative of what he 'said' about himself.

One thing that I have learned and will adjust in my life is that it is great that I love Jesus at the level that I do, as I desire to be more like Him. But, I need to be a gangster in Christ to better reflect whose I am because being naïve is not part of my history or background. What I learned by attending House of Ruth counseling was that Domestic Violence entails physical, verbal, emotional, economic, and sexual abuse. This counselor taught me in my initial consultation that I was a victim under verbal, emotional and economic abuse. I sat there in amazement because I just never applied any of this to me, no, not me! Wow I thought, as she kept talking and telling me that I certainly qualify for the sessions and we set the date and times for the follow-ups. Pastor Mike has talked about being a gangster for Christ, but I must revisit this and apply it as I am no punk and never want to be seen as one, but I must be Godly in my daily walk in order to please Him. So, finding that happy medium of never letting this happen to me again, and yet letting a man be a man without me taking his position is what I must learn to do, even better than before.

Your War Room can be wherever you want it to be, but everyone should have one if you're trying to get God's work done on the earth. Why, you may ask, well Satan is going to come after you with a vengeance and ideally it won't be through your husband, but it could be your child, your parents, your extended family and even your friends. As Pastor Mike says in the first book of his tri-part book series "you must prepare BEFORE the storm comes."

CHAPTER ELEVEN

LEANING IN ON OTHERS

Another book that I revisited was Dr. Mike's "Before the Storm." I chose this book instead of During the Storm because I wanted to be able to pat myself on the back in saying "I am prepared," and I was, Glory to God. Since I became a partner in 2009, I am equipped, as I am a doer of the Word, not just a hearer. Now, am I perfect? No, but as my Pastor says all the time, I am working on it! You see, I gave the United States Marine Corps ten years of my life and I learned to follow instructions, even when I didn't want to, as I wanted to improve my life and become better. Well, what SOFCC does for me is the same. It is Bible Based Bootcamp as Pastor Mike can be very, well raw, downright abrasive about teaching the Word of God. But, I receive as I know he is only trying to make me better. His personality is not for everyone, but perfect for me, as I am never offended by him. I embrace it as I know he is only telling me what I need to hear. I don't need passive aggressive behavior; I want the facts and the truth as I can do something with that. I am smiling as I write this but when he 'goes straight off' because audio ain't right, or the spirit is pulling on him for the people, I love it! Why, because my attitude is like his, get it right! Again, once a Marine, always a Marine and failure is not an option.

Now, I never thought I would ask to meet with Dr. DeeDee because we are just two different types of women. With that, when I met with her, I immediately went into some tears as I began to tell her that I wanted to save my marriage, as she did with Pastor Mike. God intervened and she was pulled out of her office for Dr. Mike ... truly heaven sent. When she got back, I was ready, I mean ready to share my concerns and to have an intelligent, not emotional discussion with her on what I was dealing with. When the stepdaughter was living with us, as we went to church (rain, sleet or snow), she had to go to church, and she never challenged that. However, as Pastor Mike would share aspects of himself, she and I would look at each other recognizing that her dad had many of these negative attributes of Pastor Mike's past. With that, I loved the discussions as I would hope it would penetrate, but instead when we got in the car, all the enemy would do was inform me and his daughter of what we needed to change and adjust. For the first year of this, I felt his feedback was to improve us; however, I learned that, he was simply not receiving anything for himself even when the Pastor was talking directly to him ... Satan is a trip as he can really jack up your mind, if you let him.

But, I heard Dr. DeeDee's input in our session and at that time I informed her of my story and shared photos of me to show her who I once was and hence, the additional challenges I could potentially have in marriage. She told me one major thing ... make sure he knows you need him! Umm, I thought, I know I don't do a good job of that as I am the 'get it done' chick. But I was able to remember how much I requested his support on matters of business or doing things around the house and always, and I do mean always, the television took precedence and his lovely daughter would jump in and assist me. (That dude refused to let go of that 'stupid tube' despite my input or the Pastors ... don't spend too much time in front of a television.) His daughter was such a support to me that when my company had its first year of profit, I provided her a check to pay for all her services ... as a consultant to me during the hard times. Guess what, she used it to buy a home and sho nuff blessed my life with that move. BAM! So, I did lean in on Dr. DeeDee's direct feed and unfortunately, no changes from him, and so I stayed the course and continued to pray for him as if he was acting like he was supposed to act, despite what it looked like.

Sadly, the devil informed my enemy that he did not need Bible study, so I always went by myself unless it was Corporate Prayer Night. Oh, and on these days, I would have thought he would run to the microphone to pray, but in those 6.5 years, not one time did he go up to pray. However, he was forever jumping in to pray for those around us (my friends) and was excellent at using the Word of God for those in need, I just thought, that's odd. Now, I know exactly why he didn't ... Satan told him not to and he listened!

I enjoy Pastor DeWayne's teachings every single time, and I do mean every time; I leave with new information on living out this life on earth. On a side note, it was great to see my friend Sandi's husband in church with her, as he belonged to another church and never joined SOFCC, but he loved Pastor DeWayne's teachings. Again, there is someone for everybody! Now he is my 10 am church location Pastor in Baltimore, where I now attend Sunday service. Yes, I miss attending the 10 am service in Brandywine, but I am closer to Baltimore and emotionally it is good for me as I don't revisit my life as a married woman amongst other single and married couples that attend that location, as I don't see those individuals every week.

I must talk about Pastor Deborah Grant, as that is one praying and teaching woman. She has always blessed my life with her prophetic word and the words of wisdom she shared whenever she taught. Her family stories are always fun and humorous. I have always received when she shared with the SOFCC partners and so glad to see her now on Facebook regularly teaching the Word and has earned the title of Pastor. So deserving and anointed.

Another SOFCC partner that has truly been a blessing to me is Fredricia Cunegin, who approached me one day after service many years ago just to tell me that she enjoys watching me praise the Lord from her position on the Praise and Worship team. Since we're both business owners, we made a connection and have been connected since that date.

The CEO Experience is a place for Christian Business owners to come together once a month to discuss business based on the Word of God. Now, I certainly don't want to brag, but thanks to SOFCC and the teachings (not preaching) of the Word, I am operating at a high level of being a young business owner and being a Christian. One of the first things I learned that I was excited about was the subject on doing business with others in negotiations. The facilitator walked us through the mindset of coming to the table – others minded. Well, this is who I am and yet, I was surprised to see that several at the table were challenged with this discussion. When we have discussed how to work with conflict in the office space, I was surprised how some at the table have difficulty facing conflict. Whereas, despite how uncomfortable it is, I know that matters at work must be addressed and as an owner, I realize the importance of ensuring that conflicts in the office must be managed quickly to prevent Satan's tricks from spreading.

Oh, and when the attack happened, I had the opportunity to show others in our group of my belief in FAITH and trusting God because my enemy requested the house, a percentage of the business, alimony, a car and my Tempur-Pedic mattress. A few of them were concerned that he may get these items based on the divorce laws, but my answer was "I have what I say" and Satan cannot win.

You see, at the CEO Experience it is all about being a Christian and a business owner. The founder, Ken Gosnell, is a great leader and he uses the Word of God to enhance himself and others to be good stewards of their life and the life of others as business owners. We take one day a month to sit down and focus on what the Bible has to say about running a business and I always leave satisfied with new nuggets in living my life for God as a serial entrepreneur. We also talk about anything with our team and since our Rockville team is all women (not purposeful), I did share my matters with them, and they surrounded me in prayer and sanctification. You see, since I have employees, the weight of keeping them employed and paying them was a lot and having these women who understood that aspect of the attack on my life was undeniably favorable to me. I will forever be grateful for each of them and their kindness towards me.

My business mentor, Lisa, who has been in business for over 22 years was and still is a great blessing in my life and my business. At this point we are friends and we mentor each other on different topics as a good mentor/mentee relationship should go. Well, the attack on my life and business was not a good experience for a woman who was admiring her walk in loving God, and honoring her husband despite his behavior, including the matter of how we were married. With that, to have this marriage destroyed based on jealousy, greed, and ego was a lot for her as she cussed and fussed about my enemy. Worst yet, my enemy contacted my fond mentor and left a message on her business phone line in order to disgrace my name and reputation. Although, all he did was add strength to my relationship with her because sadly she saw him as what he was despite my actions to cover for him. The one thing she said that was true "at least he showed his true colors this early in the success of your business, as your business is not worth anything." She is a Marine like me, and she doesn't mix her words at all. Again, she has been running a technology business supporting the government for 22 years, so she is certainly a strong, smart and rich woman. I'm glad that she is a friend of mine. As Pastor says and I purposely live out, "you are who you hang around."

Another great friend that works for the government was devasted as she too loves the Lord and we are praying sisters, I tell you! During the attack she visited, and we were driving to Wednesday night Bible Study. She reminded me that the Word tells us that the "Joy of the Lord is Our Strength," at a time when I was not at my best with the matters of the devil. I mean, I could get angry quickly about how the legal system allows someone, anyone, to walk into the commissioner's office and falsely file a criminal charge against someone. Unbelievable! But, as I shared the devasting actions like, "he changed the lock on the United States Postal Service mailbox; he accused me of stealing a chair from my own home; he accused me of stealing his items from my home when the courts had already ordered him out, and so much more, she maintained calmness. She said "Laurie, the joy of the Lord is your strength" and I looked at her calmness and shut my mouth. Only to give Him thanks for his goodness and mercy toward me! She also shared with me, the enemy *forgot* that you were the conduit for him and his family and listening to the devil has negatively impacted the blessings for his children's children.

Cheryl Thompson and I got closer during this time, in a way that I didn't think was possible. I have always admired her as a professional Black woman. She had patience, integrity and loyalty that was visible, as I once worked with her over 15 years ago. But this was rough on her, and I could see that as she thought about her challenges in life while I was going through my biggest challenge. This meant to me that she was feeling doubly attacked and when Satan told the enemy to go after her integrity, she was upset, and she probably still is if it's brought up (Cheryl, don't read this – smile). I prayed for her, as I prayed for the others, but I had some heaviness at times when I left her, as I could see the weight she was carrying. Thank God, she held on and made it through with me, and she is already seeing double for her trouble!

Chatting with #2 of CivilityMS, Cheryl Thompson and my leader in Business Development, Mario Walker in the background

CHAPTER TWELVE

FAITH AND PATIENCE

Faith ... is it real, or not? I am here to tell you that it is, and if you're reading this book and you have been blessed to connect with a Pastor that teaches Faith, awesome! Lean in on that teaching and study the Word, test it and see that it is real. If you are not, get ready for a head-spinning experience when you make the adjustment to have FAITH in every area of your life. I am telling you, this book that says "As My Leaders Go ... So Do I" comes from my Pastor, Apostle Mike Freeman of SOFCC. He says this to us whenever he testifies of the goodness of Jesus in his life, Dr. DeeDee's life and their family.

However, I established this chapter just to give insight on my one on one discussion with Apostle Mike Freeman. You see, I had already met him after service and learned that the enemy had requested his tithes and offerings back, but now I wanted to share with him an update on my frustrations. The legal system, oh my God, was working me even more than the continuous antics of the enemy. So, I shared my frustrations and the concern of others regarding my attorney, as no one understood why this was happening and why the courts wouldn't simply fix it. Specifically, the fact that I was living outside my home, with the law protecting him, and it was my home, in my name, and my mortgage. Well, Pastor calmly leaned back in his chair after I assured him that I had Faith for the process and said, "Laurie, Faith and Patience is what the scripture says we must use," and at this moment the room stood still for me ... and I received! From that point on, I calmed myself from the anxiety I had with the unknowns, and focused on doing my part, legally, to regain control over my life.

Another major concern for me regarding a divorce was needing to tell my Pastors who minister over and over that "Divorce is not an option," that I was getting a divorce. My spouse and I talked the talk of SOFCC, that "Divorce was not an option." During six years of the marriage, we declared and decreed those words and really meant them. We knew the Bible was our answer. Our marriage was based on the Bible as we: 1) did not have sex before marriage; 2) had counseling sessions; 3) reviewed each other's credit reports; 4) had him vetted by a federal police officer; 5) told my pastor, and he answered the call to my desires of a husband. Checking these boxes, and having two great examples before me, and being able to check off all my required attributes...I knew this was going to be the man that I would be married to for the rest of my life. Whew, here I go God doing it your way and winning, let's just walk this out and be a light for others.

Based on what was happening to me by the person that was to protect me, the person that made me whole in the eyes of living the Proverbs 31 life, I was in awe that he became my #1 enemy. I knew I was getting a divorce as I needed to ensure that I wouldn't ultimately end up in jail by 'snapping' one day. Also, he enjoyed Dateline, and if you know anything about that show, it is all about someone being killed in some concealing, but yet innocent way. In every case, the wealthy person was killed by a spouse or family member, ummm. I certainly didn't want to become a headliner for the Dateline program! But, thank God for Dr. DeeDee who said to me "you were fine before him and you will be fine after him." Talk about a load coming off me, yes, yes, yes. I was like a child and my mom had given me instruction. So now, I not only had Faith and Patience, but I was ready for the fight.

I had to go back to my past victories often to get through, and the Bible instructs us to do so as David did when he was confronting his biggest battle against the giant. I had the victory of leaving the LGBTQ community; victory of leaving the kitchen table and now being in a 3,000 square foot office; and victory of investing in real estate to name a few. I recall the story that Pastor Mike shared about him and Dr. DeeDee going into shopping centers looking at clothing that they could not yet afford. To paraphrase, let me just say that Pastor Mike broke down and purchased an expensive outfit for Dr. DeeDee and the story ends with her now being able to shop wherever she pleases. Well, as this book is titled 'As My Leaders Go ... So Do I,' here's why.

I went into a St. John's store in the Chesapeake Outlet, when I was still sitting at that kitchen table paying myself $7.50 an hour as President and CEO of CivilityMS. I had admired seeing first ladies, and now successful women business owners wearing St. John shoes or clothing. I wanted some of that in my closet. I wear glasses, especially if I need to read something. So, I am in this store without my glasses (not purposely done), and it was a blessing as I couldn't see the prices, but I got the chance to see that St. John's clothing had more style than I thought. I was excited and walked around enjoying all the beautiful colors and different styles. So, of course one of the sales ladies came to check in on me to assist me with any needs and I stated, "No ma'am, not at this time." I continued to peruse the store and not one time did I look at the price tag, and heck I couldn't see it anyway. After 15 – 20 minutes I was leaving out and the lady asked for my email address so that she could send me announcements of sales, etc., of course I said. Well, I began to get those emails and oh my, I was shocked when I saw the prices ... WHAT??? I must tell you that today I have so many pieces in my closet that I can't give you a count; however, that lady has become my friend and she calls me whenever new items come in. As I said, "As My Leaders Go ... So Do I."

There were several times that I was flowing with the Pastor, and many times that he stood before me at the Brandywine location, as if he was talking just to me. I recall when he was telling the story of going to the Bahamas with the leaders of SOFCC in order to ensure that the team was in total agreement of the direction of the ministry and he was reporting that he was so glad that he had a solid team. He then shifted and shared something like "some of you have folks on your team that need to go, and you need to fix it now." Well, I was experiencing this, and it was having an affect on the entire team as this one individual loves God but was not understanding the real damage that was happening to the company and the employees of CivilityMS at that time. Before that week was out, this matter was resolved, and God is faithful as his hand was inserted to assist with the means to bring it to an end.

Then there was a day that Pastor was teaching and walking the pulpit and he was sharing how we need to keep standing even when it's tough. Then he stopped right in front of me and said, "To be honest, you are scared and don't know what is going to happen" then he reached out his hand and said, "it's already alright." I received and cried in the pew like a baby for once again the Lord gave me strength through my Pastor. It does really matter what church you belong to!

Oh, and don't let me forget the statement that Pastor Mike shared before he began teaching, as both him and Dr. DeeDee were in the pulpit. He talked about Same Sex Marriages and that we must be careful how we embrace what the world is throwing our way on this matter. He noted that it is now in television programs, commercials and that we must remember what the Word says about same sex relations. But more importantly, he was clear that this is not his determination, but that he must stand on what the Word say's on all matters of how we are to live out our lives. I began to tear up, but I did not drop my head because I fought the thoughts, but let's be clear that once again I found myself questioning whose I am. At this time, I had informed not one but two young ladies that I would not become their husband/wife, as I love the Lord and wanted to follow Him and his principles for my life. One of these young ladies had not contacted me in over 5 years, and now that I am separated headed toward divorce, she calls me with stories of dreams, thoughts, etc. Well, once she learned that I was heading toward divorce, she was clear in saying "Laurie it will never work with you and men, you and I are supposed to be together" and as much as I felt her pain of her not being with me, I had to stand on the Word.

The second lady saw me on a panel and claimed me. What I didn't like about this one is that she should have not been able to see that I 'once' lived that life, but she did. That shook me up a bit, as I knew then that as much as I have changed, there were still signs that another lesbian could see or hear from me. You see that mind is something else and Satan is a trickster. He is always at work and yes, this is exactly what happened after the first failed marriage ... but I know too much now! We must really monitor our mind for the Lord.

To have Pastor Mike share this during announcements was just for me. I shouted out "Glory to God," and Pastor let the church marinate as you could hear a pin drop for a moment or so after I shouted. I have continued to thank God for his Word in due season, as I have not meditated or discussed this matter since that day.

Practicing the Word of God in the area of faith and patience is rewarding beyond measure, because if you live this life on purpose with full intent, you too can be rewarded by having what you say. This is another statement that I say often "I have what I say." Along with thanking God just because, as I don't know what He is up to, I just know I am in on whatever He has for me. I am constantly learning that He's got my back and with that I can go out and share with whomever that they need to have the Lord in their life, and I do it solely by testifying. You see, I have not yet gotten comfortable with praying the prayer of salvation with folks that I meet but testifying about his goodness is natural and freeing for me, and I leave them trusting that their heart has been pierced with my words.

The #1 man that can speak into my life ... my Pastor, Apostle Mike Freeman of SOFCC

CHAPTER THIRTEEN

FIGHT THE FIGHT

The fight is fixed ... We Win! But remembering that each time, every time, that your thoughts will be challenged, was the real challenge. You know Satan is a trickster, and his efforts will always pull you to go against God's word. The court rooms of Prince George's County were where my challenge was the most. Despite my enemy's attacks on me and my peeps, he had mastered the legal system very well and manipulated it by striking all the right cords. Now, I had to learn how to play in this legal territory that I had avoided for many years.

When I reflect on my first experience with the law, I remember when I had to have my favorite candy, and I wanted to get enough to share and have some for later. It was Starbursts assorted candy, and one of the 'newer' candies in the store. So, I had been in this local store that was about a 30-minute walk from our home and I decided to stop by before heading to school. I was by myself; I don't recall having any of my friends with me, but I eyed the large bag of

Starbursts candy and worked the store as I had in the past when I stole items from them; but this was different, as the bag was big, but I had to have it. With that, I felt I had found the best hiding spot in the store to tuck it away under my shirt and within the seam of my pants, but as soon as I pulled my shirt down the owner of the store came around the corner of the aisle. I was guilty and I know I looked like it and commenced to run and he caught me, pulled up my shirt and 'voila', candy bag! The owner took me to his office, and he was furious and called the Calumet Park Police. You see the store was across the street from the Chicago line, and now I am dealing with a small suburb, a white small suburb; that is not a good place for us black folks, especially since we were seen as the new problem to their neighborhood.

The police came, and I was about 11 years of age and they handcuffed me and placed me in the back of the police car. In my mind I knew I was in big trouble, not with the po po, but with my Dad. He was going to kill me! Despite the bad criminal acts of his kids, mom covered us so well, specifically my brothers as she had 'cleaned' it all up before Dad had gotten home. But, heck, I am handcuffed and going to jail and don't know how long it will be before I get out and oh my God ... Dad is going to kill me! My Catholic minded Dad believed in whoopings, beatings, whatever term you want to use in order to make it clear that the behavior was unacceptable. But, without any excuse, me and my brothers were a product of our environment and he was off working hard to make the money for us to survive, and we were doing our "thang." Well, once I arrived at the Police Station it was 'all eyes on me' and they all made me feel guilty of my act because this 'all white' team of folks, including the white women in civilian attire stared at me and called me nigga girl. Amazingly, I was not afraid of them at this young age, because I had only seen them as evil, mean folks anyhow. I was taken to processing, and they took my gym shoestrings stating, "we don't want you down there trying to hang yourself, do we?' and walked me down these dark stairs and placed me in a jail cell. Now, I have no idea how long I was in that cell, but I was cold and confused as I didn't understand what was going to happen. I was not allowed to call anyone; I was just processed as a thief (which I was) and placed in a cell.

Since I was the only one down there, it was very lonely and quiet, until I heard a man shouting and screaming at folks. The voice got louder and closer to me and the closer he got to me I realized he was rebuking the staff for placing me (a minor) in a cell and treating me like an adult. Well, to my relief, he opened the cell, apologized and asked me if I was ok. He then took me upstairs and provided me with my shoestrings and jacket. He then asked me if I had someone to call and I told him "yes, my mom" and he allowed me to call her and she came to pick me up. Just as my mom had protected my brothers, she also protected me, as I was able to get home before my brothers and friends were out of school; however, some folks saw me get hauled off in the police car and the word certainly got around in school. Oh well, it just gave me some street cred, which is always good in the hood.

Second and most importantly, as a young girl, I watched my brothers run the projects I resided in, and my dad was a man that was not going to tolerate any disrespect ... from anyone! So, as a black woman that served in the United States Marine Corps in the early eighties, I was prepared for the rough times that I would encounter, specifically from men. You see, I was taught in my home to take a stand for myself; whereas, you couldn't just say anything to me, you certainly couldn't touch me inappropriately without an immediate reaction from me.

Wow, I just remembered another story that is something else now as I think about it, but there was so much going on, as others around me that loved me were staying on top of the matters as they arose. Well, when I finally got back into my home, one of my military buddies came to stay the night with me, as I was not allowed to have any guns based on the protective order that was in place, not even in my home. Well, my retired Army buddy, Michelle, came on through and slept on my couch that night prepared for the enemy should he be foolish enough to come by ranting and raving like a crazy man. Um, um, um, some of the stories that can be told about this part of my life. Too much!

So, when I joined the Marine Corps there was much sexual harassment, but I didn't consider it that, I just thought they were stupid dudes that had no idea who they were talking to.

I am forever grateful for my parents who were good looking folks, and they blessed me with their DNA. I was not anything like my mom, but more like my dad, intolerant to disrespect. So, when guys stepped out of line with trying to 'rap' with me, they got an earful! I remember one time when walking to the chow hall (dining room) with my two buddies and several guys were on the balcony of the barracks screaming down at us. Well, after I had heard enough, I turned and headed directly for them, challenging them to bring their butts down and say it to my face. Along with that, I began to signify (what Chicagoan's called instigating) and talked about them, their mama, their daddy and anyone else in order to demean them. In the meantime, my buddies, one from New Orleans and the other from Connecticut is calling and pulling on me, Laurie let's go! But I had to give them a piece of my mind and there was no stopping that, ump. What a shame!!!

Well, when the attack happened and I learned that my spouse fraudulently charged me with 2nd degree assault, his intentions were to have me jailed for seven years. WHAT????? Yes, that was his intentions and I had to hear it repeatedly in my face, in voice mails, emails and text messages. It was a lot for me to handle as I was accustomed to protecting myself as necessary. But Satan's strategy was a good one because some that know me could think that I would and could assault someone. However, I don't and have never attacked a person, I just know if you come for me, I have something for you!

To be totally transparent, I have a tough demeanor and when I served in the Corps I often heard from the fellas, "Laurie, I thought you were a B___H, but you're way cool." Well, I was unaware of my swag of total confidence. I stand 5'9" tall and have been fit most of my life and have never experienced low self-esteem, just the consistent desire to be better. With that said, many folks that know me could question "did Laurie viciously and savagely beat her husband?" These are the words that I read on the complaint to the Commissioner's office in Prince George's County, and I was shocked to say the least. However, beyond being a woman in the Marine Corps, I also studied boxing as a workout, long before there was a Laila Ali who brought women boxers to the forefront in 1999. Not only was I totally impressed with this movement, but she was stunning and bad in that ring. Now, I had some of the fella's in the gym telling me that I should consider boxing professionally ... ah, no! My response was "really, I am approaching 40 years old and ain't no way I am going to start boxing and jack up my face!" I giggle as I think of this statement, because I knew my facial expression to those dudes was clearer than my comments. But you better believe that I became a follower of her and other women that had begun to box, as I loved me some Muhammad Ali as a child.

The courts were where the real fight was for me as I don't care for the legal system in this country. Why, you may ask? Well, just look at the history of black people and the court system. It doesn't matter whether I did it or not, I could go to jail. You see, after being involved with illegal distribution, illegal activities with marketing women and other criminal acts, the last thing I found acceptable was going to jail for something that I did not do! That was a lot for me every day because I had worked so hard to live this great life for the Lord only to have someone manipulate my life story to my disadvantage. Oh, and when my status as a Woman Marine was challenged, the hairs on my head stood up ... I can laugh and smile about this now, but at that moment, oh my, I wanted to get in their face!

So, after having way too many defeats in the courtroom, this day I was so angered that once the judge excused us, I followed the enemy out of the court room, with no intentions, I just wanted him to know I wasn't scared of him. However, everyone else knew this was not a good idea and as always, I had my crew with me in courts and they reacted to me being right up on him in courts by yelling "Laurie, stop!" When he turned around, I was no more than 3 feet from him and he panicked and screamed out help, help (like a punk). Now, he is not a little man, neither was he afraid, but I sadly aided to his efforts of claiming me as violent. I am not violent, but I am NOT a punk! Well, when I chatted with Pastor Dewayne later in the day, totally upset that once again the courts had failed me, he let me know that he knew of my move at the courts. So, I had to settle down and take the lesson from the Assistant Pastor (but he is really like a Big Brother to me) of SOFCC. He scolded me 'nicely', but he was clear, "Laurie stay away from him."

AS MY LEADERS GO...SO DO I

CHAPTER FOURTEEN

DON'T EVER GIVE UP

Write the vision, make it plain, is what supported me in creating a vision board shortly after sitting at my kitchen table to establish CivilityMS in 2012. Unbeknownst to me that's where I would spend most days from morning to night for approximately 4.5 years, sitting in front of this vision board. To establish CivilityMS, I needed to jump off the roof and not be employed by another company, as I wanted to self-certify as a Woman Owned Small Business (WOSB) and it required you to not work for anyone during 'normal business hours.' Hence, I waited to self-certify with the Small Business Administration (SBA) to ensure that I operated in integrity ... from the start!

With that, after my contract ended with supporting NASA Headquarters, I focused solely on building CivilityMS. During this time, I watched my enemy go in and out of jobs and produced little to nothing, as the work was in sales. I had to always hear the stories of what 'someone' else was doing that prevented him for maintaining employment. However, I stayed the course of running up and down the highways of the DC Metropolitan area shaking hands and getting to know others and letting them get to know me. There were a few times that someone said to me "Laurie you can do this because you are married." I fought hard to be respectful of my husband and never gave anyone the impression that I was the one holding it down in my household, not my husband. These times would always lead me to pray for him to be blessed so that he could be who God called him to be. I kept the faith and kept the Word in my heart and as I drove home, it would be CD time, as I kept feeding my mind what I needed, when I needed it.

Having a business plan in place, serves me well even today because despite the attacks I have had to overcome as it is a reference point of what I see happening 'still' in my life and the life of CivilityMS. Being an entrepreneur is not easy, as it requires you to take risks ... every single day! My enemy grew impatient and recommended that I go back to work, which shocked me initially as that totally was a sign of defeat and I refused to be defeated in developing CivilityMS. Also, I thought, "how could you, since you are not maintaining employment to help pay the bills," but I kept my mouth closed. As the Bible says and Pastor Mike says often "a woman is to keep quiet." Of course, he says it jokingly most times. Well, I actually practiced this and found myself at peace more often than my life before understanding God's word. It was just not worth a response most times! God kept me as I continued to pay my tithes and offerings while paying myself minimum wage, and once Dr. Mike spoke of sowing where you're going, I began to pay 20% of my minimum wage salary in order to show God that I truly did trust Him, and that no one else could get me through the journey of being a successful business owner that will have power and influence.

On the note of power and influence, I must share how God has shown up in this area of my life ... very powerful! Since being a business owner, I have sat on numerous panels, served as keynote speaker, and the most powerful was being asked to sit before the U.S. Senate Small Business Committee. This happened first in 2016, as I was requested to speak to Congress on Veterans Entrepreneurial Training. But this year (2019), I was asked to once again speak before Congress, but on the SBA Reauthorization Act, which addressed the small business programs that support the economically disadvantaged small businesses in this country. To later have individuals from the U.S. House of Representatives review my written testimony and call my office (yes, they called my office) and requested me to come and speak to the House of Representatives Small Business Committee, wow, what an honor! God is a faithful God, and I often say to people "I have what I say," as I did ask the Lord to have power and influence along with being a successful owner, which is also a teaching from SOFCC.

Additionally, I have received awards from the SBA SCORE office; the Department of Veteran's Affairs; the University of Maryland

University College and a few others. Many of these were awarded based on my due diligence of developing CivilityMS, not because of our revenue as there wasn't much of that. CivilityMS seemed successful long before the revenue showed up in 2016 with a $2 million-dollar contract over two years. Not to mention, the invite as a Veteran to be in the presence of the highest-ranking Veteran on Veteran's Day, Vice President Joe Biden who spent time chatting with me and it was so 'normal.' This invite happened within 24 hours after Pastor Deborah Grant prayed over Brelyn Freeman regarding her reaching higher heights, and I too received. One award in 2018, was for 1 out of 100 businesses in the DC Metropolitan area selected by the local Minority Business Enterprise, based on the revenue growth of the company. This was during the attack, along with an award for me as a Leader in my advocacy for others.

I kept the course because I consistently listened to my man of God, the leaders of SOFCC, Pastor Bill Winston, and others and not to mention tons of Praise and Worship songs. I fought my thoughts and I began to think about what I think about. Practicing the teachings from Wednesday night Bible study on "Not Being Offended" from Pastor Dewayne, years ago ... oh, what a blessing to my life. I am perfecting this area every day, as I had no college degree up until the age of 49. I knew my written and verbal communication needed improvement and was often embarrassed or offended by the reactions of others when I misspoke.

I often call upon the Lord, I mean a loud outburst, in order to get me through that moment. I am not a quiet person when I pray or worship the Lord and I am not ashamed of it. When I was fighting this last fight from the enemy, I was loud, and I would cry out to God to help me. My praise and worship music was on all the time in my office. It was loud and thank goodness my team embraced it, heck, most of them loved it. However, there is one gentleman that works for me, Mario, and I wasn't sure where he was with his walk with Christ. Well, when the attack happened toward the company, I found out that he was in the game. I mean, he would tell me, "I hear you in there" with a smile on his face. He too wanted me to know that he was not giving up and that he would fight this fight at my side, and he did. He has been very instrumental in ensuring that the relationships I develop resolve in a ROI (Return on Investment), and they have as he answers the call.

You see, I am building a multi-million-dollar business in government contracting, and I know I am in my set place because I have been tested. I realize that I must be up to something. You see in the Federal Government space of contracting, there are socio-economic statuses, and an earned status that is to assist the folks like me in gaining access to work within the Federal Government. One of them is Woman-owned, and the earned status of Service Disabled Veteran Owned, but it was the 8(a) program for the economically disadvantaged that SBA offers that opened the door for a direct-award to CivilityMS, and yet, opened the door for Satan to come in.

The 8(a) program worked for CivilityMS because I had spent 4.5 years pounding the pavement, getting myself and my company identifiable, as the government always says, "we do business with people we know, like and trust." This sole source, direct award came to us within three months of being certified ... great job, and Glory to God!

So, I stayed the course, but I hired my unknown enemy, and two others. DeAnna Boyd (my BFF), who I have known since 2001, and Cheryl Thompson, who I once worked with and hold in high regard since we met in 2005. So, we were rocking in the office and pulling off more certifications with the State and the local counties and adding new contracts to our portfolio through conference/logistics and training. We sub-leased a portion of an office in Hyattsville, and this is when the antics began that showed not only me, but the CivilityMS team that we had an enemy in the camp. What was most impressive was they never said a word, and yet they never changed toward me and their professionalism and focus for their work at CivilityMS was unmatched. I had two people on my team that I knew I could trust to do their jobs, and to do them well. Mind you, neither of them came from the government contracting space, but they learned what they needed from me and others and are now managing their roles with CivilityMS with excellence.

After our first year I was able to give out huge bonuses, more than I ever received from someone I worked for and that included a person who had assisted me when the enemy would not and I was determined to show them my appreciation. Shortly thereafter, CivilityMS brought on a Finance Manager, and oh my, I really needed that as it allowed me to go back out and about to inform government and other small businesses about our offerings. Whew, it was a blessing to add Dawn Ellis, a chi-town sista to the team. She came in and it was as if I had known her for years...sweet!

Shortly thereafter Mario Walker contacted me and told me that he was looking for a change and it was the best time for CivilityMS. We were needing a financial guru on our $2mm contract and his background is Finance, and he is also an Army Veteran. Then, I had a wow moment as I was able to hire the woman that prayed the prayer of salvation with me in 1999, Ms. Sandi. She was brought in to be the first person anyone would meet or speak to, and I knew she would represent CivilityMS at the highest level, a true Woman of God. Oh, may I add, I knew I was growing up in the Lord when she became a partner of SOFCC ... I knew I was living my life for God then!!!

I have confirmed that when Satan gets your mind, he will move quickly because his job is to steal, kill and destroy, and all he needs is a willing participant. Your mind and your thoughts are what you give him, and your actions will soon follow. He will run havoc if you let him and that is why the Bible instructs us to check him at the door (entryway of your mind). If you don't keep him under your feet, he will climb up that leg, cross over those genitals and stimulate that joker as he heads up to your heart and wrap himself around it and by that time he can easily land in your mind. As we all know from the Bible, pride is a huge entry point for him and all his tricks of wicked behavior. When someone becomes prideful, jealous and envious of you, you will certainly have an enemy, it doesn't matter who that person is or who that person was to you. She/he is now your #1 enemy!

So, when the attacks began, I lost it as I immediately put on the Chicago, Marine Corps, Dyke mindset. I was ready to rumble and take back what the enemy had stolen from me, but thanks to a dynamic team I had established in my office and the extended friends and family that were there for me, I held the course of being on God's side. As I berated the Prince George's County Legal System that the enemy now forced me to deal with, I grew inpatient over the madness that had now entered my life. But every day I was able to settle myself with the Word spoken by me or my peeps. Oh, and bless God for YouTube, as I was able to sleep each and every night. How, you may ask when you have a close, very close person that has now become someone that you don't know. Well, YouTube has great uplifting videos to listen to, but to put myself to sleep I found a 37-minute clip titled "Peace of Mind" with scriptures overplaying soft harmonious music. Waking up and always acknowledging if I had to hit replay, and I must say that I was off to sleep in less than 37 minutes over that years' time, more than not.

Also, one of our attacks came from a teaming partner that decided to take our share of the work and that impacted CivilityMS financially with a decrease in revenue of 40%. Now, the business owner of the company was well aware of this type of impact on my newly established company as they had been connected to CivilityMS for the past five years. Nonetheless, I had to lay off some of my team and decrease salaries for us all at the corporate office. But oddly, my business enemy was now joining forces with my #1 enemy ... oh my, I really must be up to something! Because I walk in knowing that no one, and I mean no one can stop me if I keep trusting God, I persevered, and my team stayed alongside me and waited for the change to happen. I have understanding that no one can take anything from me that is mine. With that, I always stood on getting back what they stole from me by operating in integrity. However, when I learned from a little birdie that my two enemies were meeting, I smiled and said, "I REALLY must be up to something."

I often ran the scripture through my mind and would repeat it out loud on occasion of how God would use my enemy as my footstool. Since the attack, I can say that my team is all back on board and we are working daily to bring on more contracts; however, we have landed contracts totaling over $4 million and growing daily and have established a joint venture to begin working in Information Technology (Cybersecurity and Engineering). So yes, the Word is true, and God is using my enemy as my footstool and I am stepping hard on each step up. I am convinced that as long as I stay in God's Word and practice his principles as I am taught to do at SOFCC, I will continue to be victorious and rise to the level that God has for me. I often, and I do mean often thank the Lord for trusting me!

I am a serial entrepreneur and always have been, but now it's of wealth development. I am a woman without children, and my heart to give was there before SOFCC got their hands on me. With that, I am not challenged and like my Pastor, I am a *Giving Machine* and I have walked in that when I didn't have much, so how dangerous will I be in the eyes of enemy with wealth. Too bad satan, you can't have me as I will do whatever the Father say's I can do and will do. Beyond CivilityMS, real estate, rebirth undergarments, and Melaleuca which are sources of income that I currently have, including speaking and being an author, I look forward to adding more. Hence, it is said that you should have seven revenue streams. I already know what they are, and it will be a focus of investing in others ... also a Godly move!

I have been flowing with Pastor over the past year or so and it consistently confirms the Word that I receive from the Lord. During this time my Pastor was teaching, and he said, "I can show you better than I can tell you, and I leaped in my seat and screamed ... "say it Pastor." Once the dust settled from obtaining attorney's, court appearances, alignment of my enemies, etc., I began to say, "I will show you better than I can tell you." You see, the fact that Satan finds me of such importance, is what I had to accept. But why, you may ask? Well, I am a giver and with wealth I can bless the land. I am willing to write the check for SOFCC, Living Word (Chicago), and other ministries in order to get the Lord's work done, and that makes me an enemy of the one that comes to steal, kill and destroy. But I never gave up pushing to make this wealth possible when it was bleak and lonely, and I'd be darned if I will allow Satan to come now and steal what God has promised me.

The victories started coming in one after another in the courts, and the favor of God was showing up as CivilityMS was being awarded contracts. During this challenge, even though we had lost much in me needing to pay out over $60,000 in legal fees, repairs, and replacement purchases to fight this battle, we were still winning. Even though he wanted ownership of my company, alimony, a home, a car, and my Tempur-Pedic mattress, he did not receive any of those items. Now, I did have to give him walk-away money as the judge calls it; however, it was less than it would cost me to go to trial for the three days that my attorney requested. Yes, three days when there are no children, no property, no assets at all jointly ... but I learned, when married, they can get half. Praise God for the victory, because as a woman, it was quite humiliating to hear a man say I want this, I want that, when he knew he did nothing to earn what he wanted.

In closing out this book, I hope that you received some encouragement, motivation, insight and determination to go and make your life happen. It is all on you, as God is not a respecter of persons, and His promises are for us all, but we must receive. If you are attending a church home that makes you uncomfortable to 'give' as you pay your tithes and offerings, use it as a barometer that you may need to find another Pastor. If you are attending a church home and the Pastor makes you uncomfortable with the Word that he gives you weekly, consider why? You must find your Pastor and when you do, I promise you that God will use him or her to bless your life and then it will be no stopping the moves you are to make as you will then be in the will of the Father. He promises us a prosperous life and that is in every area of our life. I know this now and no one can change my thoughts on that. I want for everyone what I have ... FREEDOM!

Activities during the attack: (1) CivilityMS receiving award as 1 of 100 Minority and Women Owned Businesses (2) Speaker at HUD on Memorial Day honoring Gold Star Families with Garry and Yvonne Green of SOFCC (3) Panel discussion at NIH on the challenges of Women Entrepreneurs working in Federal Government Contracting (also the day a woman in the audience claimed me as her next wife)

STORIES OF WARRIORS ON THE BATTLEFIELD

I know Teruko Richardson from the first church I belonged to; however, we have built a great relationship of love and trust. I know she will speak truth to me, and I am so appreciative of her being a SOFCC partner, and also a Spirit of Faith Bible Institute (SOFBI) Graduate, which means I get a lot more from her (smile). When the attack happened on social media, she was the first person to contact me and share that she was lifting us up in prayer. She not only prayed for me, but she also serves as the photographer for CivilityMS events. God Bless you Ms. T. for your service to the world.

"We are not built to go through life challenges alone. There are benefits to having a circle of girlfriends that we can call on during the good and not so good moments in our lives; women who will rise to the occasion when we need them – regardless of how often we interact. This is how I see sisterhood, and this is the position I upheld with Laurie during her challenge. During Laurie's challenge I prayed for her, checked in just to see how she was doing, and was available whenever she wanted to share or release. I celebrated *(praised God)* for every victory she had during the process of reaching her goal. I stood by her side, along with many other friends, at court where she was once again the victor. Laurie has a beautiful spirit. I saw her recently and she was actually glowing – it is wonderful to see her spirit smiling again. She is a beautiful spirit with a giving heart – she will literally give you the shirt off her back. I know – she did it for me! As our first lady Dr. DeeDee says, which is also the title of her talk show "We are better together."

The attack on Laurie's life revealed for me just how manipulative and scheming the enemy is. I witnessed a man's behavior toward his wife become totally obnoxious as he succumbed to the thoughts that the enemy planted in his mind. He was now trying to take down the woman that he promised to love and protect at the order of the enemy. But he failed to realize that God is true to His Word, He keeps His promises to His children. No weapon formed against us shall prosper! They may be formed; however, they will not succeed because we already have the victory. WE WIN! However, there is a process that we must go through in order to reach our goal – to realize our victory. That is why we must stay the course – when the enemy is wreaking havoc in our lives we must stay in the Word, spend quality time with God, continue to go church and Bible Study as well as fellowship with like-minded people. This is how we fight our battles – this is how we stay empowered. We cannot jump ship in the middle of the storm.

No matter what we are going through, God promises to help us. In Isaiah 41:10 (MSG) He states: *Don't panic. I'm with you. There's no need to fear for I'm your God. I'll give you strength. I'll help you. I'll hold you steady, keep a firm grip on you.* So, even though we may experience severe attacks from the enemy, we must hold on to the Word of God – He has a firm grip on us. He will not leave us alone. He is always with us and sometimes His presence is evident through those He has placed in our lives – those who are our girlfriends." Laurie, you did the darn thang!

- Teruko Richardson (Ms. T)

This awesome woman of God sought me out to participate on her radio show and on a panel discussion. It was great to share CivilityMS and insight on women-owned businesses with her radio audience. Also, I sat on a panel and on a Facebook live discussion on Domestic Violence. I was asked to share some insight on Domestic Violence in the LGBTQ community. At that time, I had no idea that I was heading toward both emotional and financial abuse by my husband, which is also Domestic Violence. She served as a great listener, allowing me to vent, while giving me the silence of an engaged audience, and now we are great friends looking to do more together to fight against Domestic Violence.

"If the cycle of abuse is to end, change is necessary. We must all take responsibility for exposing abuse and getting to the root of the problem. We all play a part in removing the shame from those who are suffering." - Then Sings My Soul

The Journey

Who me? God you want me to do what? Yes you...Wow! A stage production? Wondering, pondering, still needing Confirmation, so I talk to a few girlfriends...yes girl! Great idea! Okay God. Going in scared, stepping out into the deep, I answer the call.

A message, a mission, a movement, a ministry. A 6-year journey speaking out on domestic violence against women, children and yes, men – now it's a reality. Creator of a stage play "Then Sings my Soul," a musical with a message on domestic violence. I began to write down ideas of what areas should be addressed in my script. One scene, in particular, speaks of women who are not given a fair case in court before a judge.

On behalf of battered women who are in the fight of their lives (character) attorney Katherine is about to give up because of so many cases where judges who act as if they don't even care that lives are at stake. They hand down flimsy warnings and look the other way when they see black eyes and bruised arms. They don't understand that this is an epidemic, these women are not weak, they just need a way out. "for I know the plans I have for you, plans to prosper you and not to harm you, plans to give you hope and a future" Jeremiah 29:11

God's plan brought special people into my life – I never knew how my life would be affected by meeting so many women who shared their stories on how they survived domestic violence and heard stories about women who did not survive. I'm now starting to understand more and more why I was chosen to write a stage play dealing with domestic abuse. When I started to speak out about the devastation of domestic violence and the lives that were changed forever; the hell they went through; how domestic violence is still real - people began to see how passionate I am about it.

From Trials to Triumph

You win! Is what I said to Laurie, my sister friend the day when I received her call. She needed to share her story about a domestic situation she was going through with her husband... let me stick a pin here. He presented himself as a devoted Christian; a man who attends church on a regular; a man who hears the word and knows the word. They both attended church and were looked upon as the modeled couple. So, I was taken aback when I got this call from my sister girl telling me about the abuse she was enduring and of an alleged assault she was being accused of. A husband, who even goes so far as to want her locked up in jail. We immediately began to speak victory over this demonic act of self-gratification (John 10:10 - the devil comes to steal kill and destroy, but God came so we may have abundant life).

It does matter what church you attend. SOFCC, led by Apostle Michael A. Freeman and Dr. DeeDee Freeman, is where Laurie and I met. It is from the teachings we receive from our Apostle where Laurie drew her strength, where she knew she needed to call on a few sista soldiers. When Laurie and I would talk on the phone each time it was a "what the heck is really goin on" (one of my sayings) conversation. OMG! SMH! All the time still claiming victory!

I would call Laurie periodically to check in on her - hey girl just checking... at one point she contemplated the "s" word...the devil is a liar...I gave her a song to sing by Darlene Zschech "I will live, I will not die the resurrection power of Christ alive in me and I am free in Jesus name." She would call to say got another court date, okay sis no worries, you win. Then, ring...I won! This went on for months, each time she would go to court she came out a winner. It was like the movie with Angela Bassett, 'Waiting to Exhale' walked out from court smiling. She won!

Laurie is a strong woman, her strength has even made me stronger, she's determined to stay on the path of "I win." You may be down, but not out, you may feel weak, but yet you're strong, you may cry many tears, but have no fear...God knows, and he cares, trust the promise. An affirmation from my stage play – "still a strong woman," and yes, your soul can sing again!

- Wyomme Pariss

Dawn Ellis is the most mild-mannered, tempered woman I know. She is from my hometown, Chicago, and does not represent a hood life like me and my other home girls (good for her). But her strength is clear and present all the time. I was blessed to have her join CivilityMS as the Finance Manager, and after a few months of training, she has taken on the position and grown with it as we have grown ... love you Dawn, and don't you ever try to leave me!!

When Laurie offered me a job without even knowing me, I knew I would be indebted to this woman. She accepted me on the recommendation of a friend, and I knew that I would do anything for her to show my gratitude. The time came about eight months later when I would have to put those words into action.

One rainy Saturday afternoon as I walked around Michaels talking on the phone to Maria, my girlfriend in Chicago, Laurie called me on my cell phone (which was rare) with an urgency in her voice. She said she needed to come by and speak to me right away. Of course, I said calmly "okay", but I was in panic mode! What could she want? And what was so important that it couldn't wait until Monday? I went back to Maria on the other line and told her what had just happened. She immediately said, "Aww Dawn, I'm so sorry" as if I had just said someone died. She asked, "What could she want?", I said "I don't know, she just said that she was leaving the job and she was coming right over to talk to me." I told my friend she probably saw that I hadn't processed my transactions in QuickBooks in a timely manner or maybe I'm not working out as her Finance Manager. Either way we concluded that Laurie was coming over to fire me because in Maryland they prefer to fire people on the weekends so they can clean their things out. It's funny how our minds think of the worst possible scenarios.

I told Maria I had to go because Laurie would be arriving any moment. She said if she didn't hear from me within 30 minutes, she would start packing up the car, which I didn't doubt. When Laurie arrived, I tried to read her face, but I just saw seriousness, which could confirm mine and Maria's theory. She sat down and chatted about what was going on in her personal life and I sat listening anxiously waiting for the bomb to drop. Suddenly, she asked me if she could move in with me until she was able to get back into her house? That's it!! That's all you wanted? Again, without hesitation, I said okay. At that point, she could have asked for my bedroom and breakfast in bed! I never felt so relieved. After we spoke for a while longer, she left and I was sitting there thinking ... having my boss as a roommate, yikes!

I tried to make her as comfortable as possible, but I knew she just wanted to be back in her own home. Even the strongest person has weak moments; sometimes I would hear her weeping at night, and I would lay there and pray that God would fight this battle for her and keep her strong while she went through the process.

Life as we knew it was changing; the peace and joy that rested in our office was dissipating. I did not feel that warm and fuzzy feeling anymore and for the first time in a year, I dreaded going to work. Over the course of one year, the trials that we faced personally and professionally were almost too much to bear, but the Word assures us that no weapon formed against us would prosper and that's what we held on to. We girded our leader with prayer and positivity, and we made ourselves available to her for whatever she needed. Now, the clouds have lifted, and the storm has passed, and we can proudly say…WE WIN!!!

"God is our refuge and strength, an ever-present help in times of trouble"
Psalms 46:1

- Dawn Ellis, Finance Manager

I met Bud after service one day at SOFCC, as he boldly approached me and asked, "who are you?" We have been connected ever since and he serves as my company's alternate Facilities Security Officer (FSO). He and his wife Tia have been a blessing to me and immediately identified my attack as Spiritual Warfare. He gave me this scripture to remember… "Be Angry, but do not Sin." Love them!

During Laurie's most challenging season of her life, she not only had the confidence to lean on her subject matter experts to maintain her multi-million-dollar company, but she also reached out for spiritual encouragement as well.

My wife Tia and I encouraged her with scriptures from the Bible and prayed with and for her. Laurie refused to waiver from the Word of God that gave her hope, stability, and confidence during this time and the Word, gave her the needed motivation that led to her triumphant outcome.

- Pastor Norman Pryde, Alternate FS

This lady right here taught me much on being a project manager and overseeing federal government contracts. I am forever grateful for her kindness, patience, support and promotion of whose I am. Having her still connected to me is a blessing, and if Satan had his way, we would not be, but God is faithful. I do pray. as Dr. DeeDee does, for God to remove those from my life that shouldn't be, and to maintain those that I must have!

I remember Laurie when we traveled to San Francisco for work in 2011, and you shared your profound story with me. I witnessed how God was working out your life experiences and preparing you to be a "drum major" of your story, to share with others going through similar experiences. You also educate people who want to give their lives over to God but have allowed the devil to hold them hostage to their past experiences. I am glad that we met and worked together, but my only regret is that we did not form a stronger sisterhood, and I know that God will work that out in His time and awesome situation.

- Gwen Henderson

This woman of God is a true blessing to all of us that participate in the Rockville, MD - CEO Experience, which is for Christian Business Owners. She facilitates the sessions and has come to my office for my 1 hr. monthly coaching session. She was there in our office when the Sheriff came to deliver another fraudulent criminal charge by the enemy. As the police wanted privacy, I told them no need as everyone here is aware of the current situation that I am in. So, she stood and prayed as this interaction with police took place, and before she left us that day, she anointed our office and prayed for me and the team for victory ... we got it!

> *Therefore, I urge you, brothers and sisters, in view of God's mercy, to offer your bodies as a living sacrifice, holy and pleasing to God—this is your true and proper worship. 2 Do not conform to the pattern of this world but be transformed by the renewing of your mind. Then you will be able to test and approve what God's will is—his good, pleasing and perfect will. (Romans 12:1-2)*

These are the verses I think of when I think of Laurie and her journey. A journey of revelation, exploration, strength, and ultimately faith. Laurie's story shows her ability to not only adjust to new experiences, whether positive or negative, but make them the tools for her survival. Yes, sometimes the journey left scars, but Laurie's biggest, and most important step was to find a way to understand and receive the love of Jesus Christ.

This love, by the way of leaders, ministers, stewards, advisors, and caregivers, poured into Laurie the seeds that have become a powerful faith testimony that keeps her going each day. The Bible says that we must build our houses on firm foundations (Matthew 7:24-27). To build a foundation we must remember that multiple resources are utilized before the concrete is ever poured. The 'supplies' God has used with the cloud of advisors placed in Laurie's life, have led and still leads her today. I see this demonstrated in her leadership of Civility Management Solutions and know that God has much greatness left for Laurie as she continues her transformation of faith.

- Tracy Stevens
Chief Experience Officer
CEO Experience - Author

I have talked about this woman throughout this book, but I tell you, she is a mom, big sister, auntie, and close friend to me, and I will love her forever as a precious woman of God. I am so glad that God brought us together and I know she is going nowhere, and I don't want her too ... may I be able to bless her life in abundance, oh Lord!

I met Laurie Sayles, November 1, 1999; I believe that it was a divine intervention from day one, as God allowed me to share the Prayer of Salvation with her and that began the turning point in her life.

She has always been a very positive and personable individual, who has a winning smile and a magnetic personality. We were both from Chicago and that fact connected us forever. The Lord allowed me to share many things with Laurie, as I watched her transformed life. We went from, how-to walk-in heels, to how we clap our hands, lol. She still claps a little harder than most ladies, nevertheless, SHE is a Lady!

I don't believe Laurie ever meets a stranger; she makes you feel like you have known her forever. One day we were talking, and Laurie shared her goal of becoming a business owner, and she said, "I'd love to have you work for me." Fast forward to August 2017, I'm employed by my longtime friend Laurie, as her Executive Assistant, and what a wonderful environment to be a part of. We are all like family, working together for a common cause, simply to help others.

I sit at the front desk, and one day I received a call, which I must say, was the strangest call I've ever received. I acknowledged the phone line as usual, and this is what I heard, "Good morning team, Civility, this is____ and I'm calling to inform the staff that the company will be closing." The person went on to say, "I'm just warning you, that the gravy train is about to stop, and Laurie is not brave enough to tell you. I will be taking over the company, under another entity and reopening it in six months."

What the....? I thought this person had lost their mind! They went on to say, "I believe

Laurie is having a nervous breakdown and I need you all to help her understand the complexities and nuances of what's facing her." It was time to pray for sure, knowing that no weapon formed against Laurie shall prosper; the Devil IS a Liar!!! We bind every assignment unto Laurie and this office, in the name of Jesus!

A few days later there was a message left on the office voicemail stating, "good morning Team Civility, one last thing I wanted to inform you of, there is a good chance that your 8(a) SBA certification will be suspended, and your books audited." They went on to say, "Once the money train stops, Laurie isn't going to be able to pay her bills, this will affect your livelihood! She's not honest enough to inform you. I'm willing to see the company shut down, because I will personally re-open it under another entity." This is all out WAR!

I never thought one little person could create such havoc in the lives of so many people, but Satan had entered the mind of that individual and he blindly conformed and was doing everything he could to bring misery. There were so many false accusations, warrants, court-dates, and the stress was mounting, stress that none of us had ever experienced in this environment before. As we watched and prayed daily, it appeared that the enemy was winning; however, we couldn't afford to look at what we were seeing, we pressed through the stress, the pain and the tears.

It was vitally important that everyone put on the Armor of God daily, according to Ephesians 6:11-18. I typed out the scripture to ensure that everyone would know how to dress. We circled our CEO and did Spiritual Warfare at every opportunity. We were expecting things to get better, but it appeared that it was getting worse. We all did and said everything we could to encourage Laurie. We didn't want to react in anger and yet there was anger brewing. I felt so angry that I wanted to hit him with a bat. My exact words were, "I could take a bat and dislocate his head." Lord knows that exactly how I felt in the flesh... I even desired to shoot him in the knees, lol, but I had no weapon and certainly no training, but everything in me felt the desire.

One day a meeting was called and at that meeting we were all told that Laurie would have to cut our salaries in half, and that she would understand if we didn't stay with the company. That was a sad and unexpected announcement, however, our love for Laurie and the company allowed all of us to sacrifice and continue working for less. The enemy was not finished, and the fire was intensified.

Laurie is a very strong person, her training as a Marine and life's situations has made her that way, as it is a truth in most cases. However, this attack on her life, character, business and finance was really taking a toll, not only on her, but all of us. When she cried, we cried with her. We were all laid off in the next company meeting, but we vowed to continue working. One Sunday I went to church and the Pastor was sharing a life experience in which he worked for no pay. He asked the question, "how many of you would work for free?" I do believe I was the only person in the congregation with a proud lifted hand, not because I could afford to work without pay but, my friend Laurie was in trouble and needed my support physically and spiritually. We all realized that this was a battle requiring supernatural intervention! We began to intensify our prayers and exercised restraint to respond to our emotional and physical desire to avoid reacting in anger to the enemy. Suddenly all hell broke loose.

I am an intercessor. I have always known the value of prayer, because Momma instilled that in me as a child, and there was no question, IT WAS TIME TO PRAY like never before! We had a War Room behind the Red Door, which leads to Laurie's office. Laurie was always an upbeat, joyful individual, strong in the Lord as she has grown in the Word, but Satan was shaking her to the core. Everyone in the office had committed to be prayerful and cautious, but that wasn't enough. The joyful woman that I had known was becoming angry, bitter and fearful as the enemy was attacking daily and appeared to be winning. In addition to all that he had done, he was literally destroying her home! That nut took a hammer to the house. I had to call on other intercessors to pray for Laurie and the company without revealing the nightmare we were experiencing. It became more apparent that more warfare prayers were required in the office. I shared scriptures to reinforce our faith, scriptures that were heard before became more real as the battle intensified, as I prayed other's prophecies.

Our office was always unified, but now we were more unified in faith and in love. We began to surround Laurie and pray for her strength as she had begun to feel the real weight of this demonic attack. We would bind the hand of the enemy and loose the truth of God's Word to be manifested in Laurie's mind, body, spirit, soul and life. We put God in remembrance of His Word and Laurie began to rebuild her faith muscles. We bound fear, worry, doubt, and anxiety as we loosed the truth of God's Word that Laurie was an overcomer in every area of her life, more than a conquer because of the finished work at Calvary, We Always WIN, per Pastor Mike, and so we did. Thanks, Laurie, for the opportunity to share on fighting the good fight of faith.

- Sandi Goins

I was in awe of this woman when I first saw and heard her, as she was the keynote speaker on a boat ride with over 190 women veterans. She is a retired, highest ranking, enlisted black woman, who has done great things in her journey through life, including working with President Obama on veteran and military spouse initiatives. She is a bad, bad chick, and right out of Baltimore! When I started my company, she was in total support and has done trainings for CivilityMS since we were established. I love her and trust her with all that I have as she rolls like that. So glad you're in my life and I look forward to doing more great things with you.

I can't remember the exact date or day that Laurie gave me the full scope of what she was going through, but what I DO remember is what I thought "Oh, Hell NO!!" Although I was going through my own heartache and loss –I knew I had to do whatever I could to lift my sista up and be there in whatever capacity God saw fit. Besides being friends and business partners— she was my fellow sister veteran. As I like to say, she was being attacked in a most vicious campaign by "the enemy," on a campaign to destroy her by any and all means necessary, to knock her down and keep a boot on her back, because she dared to "Stand up and fire back!" Not on my watch!! What "the enemy" failed to understand is that she had an arsenal that was equipped with more ammunition than he could ever imagine - her friends. This is what friends do, be there no matter what, in whatever capacity one can. That day came.

It was when I saw "the enemy" in his true form. I do not wish to replay the details; however, it was the day I truly feared for Laurie's safety. As we sat in the courtroom waiting for her name to be called, I watched her. The fear in her eyes, her nervous chatter, unsteady hands and the way this most confident sister seemed to jump every time the courtroom door opened was a clear indication to me that she was afraid, not of the proceedings, but of "the enemy." I knew then that I would not let any harm come to her, God willing. To make matters worse, "the enemy" still had access to **her** house! There was no way that I was going to allow her to be home by herself overnight. So, as we departed from the courthouse, I told Laurie, "I'm staying over your house!" She's a strong sister make no mistake, but the fear was there-- then the relief in her eyes when I told her she was going to have an impromptu sleepover.

So, I stayed, not in one of the bedrooms, but on the couch so I could see every entry point prior to getting to her bedroom. Note, I said stayed, not slept, and being there meant being vigilant, awake and ready to do whatever was necessary for her to remain unharmed and to sleep—she was so tired. People may say I put myself at risk and that is true, but the bigger risk was leaving her alone, and that was not a risk I was willing to take.

The takeaway for any strong and fierce woman out there—we are stronger and fiercer when we lean in on others when we need to and sometimes just want to. God is always with you, but I believe HE gives us the precious gift of others here on earth. The victory is always sweeter when you have your battle buddies with you.

- Michele S. Jones, Consultant

This chick right here is my 'gurl' ... and my Chi Town homie! We have known each other for 20 years now and I would have not thought that we would be as close as we are. Why, because she is a loving wife and mother to two beautiful children, even home schooling. Whereas, I have no kids, but yet, our relationship is about each other ... no one else. Her family knows me, and she has known many of my other friends, but none of them matter, we are just cool with each other, all the way!!

Hello, my name is DeAnna, and I want to share my personal experience dealing with the attack of my BFF Laurie. I confess, this was a challenge to sit down and revisit the experience. When I was in it, it was intense and I was busy blocking attacks, shielding myself from the evil force of the attacker. The strides to stay ahead of all the lies, schemes and false charges was an emotional and physical undertaking. During this time, I was a student at Inner Visions Institute attending a two-year Personal Development program. This program was extremely supportive in keeping me in my right mind by learning the Universal Law and Spiritual Principles. Also, during most of this turbulence I was able to detach my personal emotions and focus on tackling the vicious boulders hurled our way. I leaned in with faith "The assurance of things hoped for the conviction of things not seen" Hebrews 11:1, all the while praying for our victory once we reached the other side.

I admit somedays I had to lean in harder and ask for extra prayer because the terrain was treacherous. The deadly venom that was constantly sprawled in our direction had no power to withstand the power of God. I would say to anyone reading this, trust your gut if you pick up things early on about disingenuous people. As much as I wanted to support my friends' happiness in this new relationship, I should have spoken my truth about what I was feeling. I kept my mouth closed in hopes I was wrong about judging this relationship as a mistake. If you see crazy coming warn your friend, relative, or even a co-worker to steer clear of a major wreck. The wreck can be life altering, and in some cases fatal.

This was a real-life movie with so many twists and turns. I remember the night I was casually watching the office video feed from home and I saw Laurie walking into her office. Even though it was late I didn't think much of it because she worked late hours and she could have just popped in to grab some documents. Unbeknown to me at that moment this was the beginning of a journey that included threats, numerous court dates and late-night huddles strategizing our next moves. Anyone in the office at any given time would hear gospel music, motivational speakers and praying. There was a lot of praying. Even when things didn't seem to be in our favor, I knew if I maintained a mustard seed of faith anything was possible for our good. Even in the moments when I was in the courtroom and heard taunting from the enemy, or when he looked at me and told me I would be fired from a job that he had no authority over, my livelihood was threatened, my reputation was at stake, and I kept it moving. I wanted to keep moving because there wasn't any time to rest. Laurie and I are ride to live friends to the end. The victory is ours.

I didn't fight in the beginning of this union but in the end, I fought with every spiritual tool, and when needed I added pieces of the South Side of Chicago. A little hood never hurt when you need to get someone up off you. It rolled up and evoked my "Don't get it twisted… Ain't no punk living here." Lastly, I would like to give a heartfelt thank you to my loving husband Dedric for all of his support during the time that I had to be there for my BFF, we both have much love for Laurie!

- DeAnna Boyd

Ms. Freddie, what can I say, but what a wonderful woman of God that has a spirit of love and genuine concern … for everybody who has the pleasure of knowing her. I have had deep discussions with Freddie about 'whose' I have been in car rides as we were out and about trying to drum up business and let folks know we exist. She has been both an inspiration and a great encourager in the Word, and Fasting & Praying, as I take her lead in this area of my life as well.

One Sunday morning after the 8am service, at the Temple Hills campus, Laurie and I exchanged pleasantries, conversing long enough to disclose our human resource management professional similarities; we shared a little about our respective dreams of establishing and building an organization. At that time, there were no indicators of the depth of sisterhood that brief exchange would develop.

Fast forward, we have established our own organizations, however, we've also recognized a friendship that extends beyond building dreams. I'm proud to share how I've watched Laurie build her organization and brand from grassroot beginnings, coast-to-coast, and yes even to Congress. But it does not stop there; in the past two years, Laurie has allowed me to walk with her through a shadow of death experience. It was through walking that process with my friend, that intercession, worship, decreeing and declaring God's Word, and staying focused, that we literally did see the Hand of God at every stage of the process. There were days when she would receive an unfathomable message from her enemy that sounded like a Lifetime movie scene. One of our foundational scriptures was:

Mark 11:22-24 Amplified Bible (AMP)

22 Jesus replied, "Have faith in God [constantly]. 23 I assure you *and* most solemnly say to you, whoever says to this mountain, 'Be lifted up and thrown into the sea!' and [a]does not doubt in his heart [in God's unlimited power], but believes that what he says is going to take place, it will be done for him [in accordance with God's will]. 24 For this reason I am telling you,

> whatever things you ask for in prayer [in accordance with God's will], believe [with confident trust] that you have received them, and they will be *given* to you.

This was a constant go-to scripture; and we did not waver. I recall the morning when she asked her community of friends, who also walked through many of the Lifetime scenes, to provide visible support in the court room, and we were there. It was apparent that I was not the only one who was praying and ultimately present, when the Judge dismissed the case. I watched my friend lean against another dear friend and wept. For every hurdle Laurie had to jump, she would say, "I trust God," and without hesitation, she jumped every hurdle, even the ones that seemed to grow like weeds. Laurie was clear that she had to execute the faith upon which she stood then and continues to stand today.

Laurie, congratulations! I'm proud to call you my friend. And while you always knew that the battle was won, you now have many trophies of success – the accomplished hurdles – to remind you, and share with others through this manuscript, that God never fails.

- Minister Fredricia Cunegin,
MSM, PHR, SHRM-CP
President/CEO
HRinMotion LLC

(1) Victory Lunch after dismissal of criminal assault charge
(2) My support at courthouse with me and my attorney, Charles Walton, Esq. the day my assault case was dismissed

Civility Management Solutions

Laurie Sayles – President and CEO

Civility Management Solutions

9111 Edmonston Road, Suite 302

Greenbelt, MD 20770

301-352-7875

WWW.CIVILITYMS.COM

Laurie@civilityms.com

R3 Nonprofit Founder

info@RCLLC.org

240-206-6022

www.ingramcontent.com/pod-product-compliance
Ingram Content Group UK Ltd.
Pitfield, Milton Keynes, MK11 3LW, UK
UKHW061139180426
11947UKWH00001B/1